D0146131

# AMAZING GRACE

# AMAZING GRACE

## *AFRICAN AMERICAN GRANDMOTHERS AS CAREGIVERS AND CONVEYORS OF TRADITIONAL VALUES*

DOROTHY SMITH RUIZ

Foreword by Bert Hayslip

Westport, Connecticut
London

Library of Congress Cataloging-in-Publication Data

Ruiz, Dorothy S. (Dorothy Smith)
    Amazing grace : African American grandmothers as caregivers and conveyors
of traditional values / Dorothy Smith Ruiz ; foreword by Bert Hayslip.
        p. cm.
    Includes bibliographical references and index.
    ISBN 0–275–98077–4 (alk. paper)
    1. Grandparents as parents—United States.   2. African American grandmothers.
I. Title.
        HQ759.9.R85 2004
        306.874'5'08996073—dc22          2004044377

British Library Cataloguing in Publication Data is available.

Copyright © 2004 by Dorothy Smith Ruiz

All rights reserved. No portion of this book may be
reproduced, by any process or technique, without the
express written consent of the publisher.

Library of Congress Catalog Card Number: 2004044377
ISBN: 0–275–98077–4

First published in 2004

Praeger Publishers, 88 Post Road West, Westport, CT 06881
An imprint of Greenwood Publishing Group, Inc.
www.praeger.com

Printed in the United States of America

The paper used in this book complies with the
Permanent Paper Standard issued by the National
Information Standards Organization (Z39.48–1984).

10  9  8  7  6  5  4  3  2  1

To my sons, Jason and Alex, for their constant support.
To my mother, Mary Brinson Smith, for her love and kindness.
To my late father, Willie L. Smith, for his strength and integrity.

To my late great aunt, Ruby Lee Smith, who taught me
the value of lifelong learning.
To all custodial grandmothers, for their devotion to family
and love of children.
To all elders who have influenced and inspired me with
their wisdom.

## AMAZING GRACE

*T'was Grace that taught . . .*
*my heart to fear.*
*And Grace, my fears relieved.*
*How precious did that Grace appear . . .*
*the hour I first believed.*

*Through many dangers, toils and snares . . .*
*we have already come.*
*T'was Grace that brought us safe thus far . . .*
*and Grace will lead us home.*

*When we've been here ten thousand years . . .*
*bright shining as the sun.*
*We've no less days to sing God's praise . . .*
*than when we've first begun.*

# Contents

# Foreword

Growing out of the awareness that diversity best characterizes middle-aged and older adults, our attention to those dimensions that define custodial grandparents has deepened our understanding of the challenges and rewards of raising a grandchild. Grandparents raising grandchildren can be differentiated along a number of parameters: age, gender, urban-rural place of residence, marital status, and race/ethnicity. The most salient of these parameters is that of race/ethnicity, and in this light, much has been written with regard to the caregiving experience of African Americans, most of whom are women. Over the last decade, the work of Meredith Minkler and that of Linda Burton has provided the most insight into such grandparents' lives. *Amazing Grace: African American Grandmothers as Caregivers and Conveyers of Traditional Custodial Values* emerges as another milestone in this respect, building on the above with in-depth projects focusing on African American grandmothers raising their grandchildren.

Among its unique features, *Amazing Grace* puts custodial grandparenting into historical context, and presents quantitative findings regarding both physical and mental health and factors influencing custodial grandmothers' life satisfaction and depression. Most importantly, however, *Amazing Grace* presents qualitative data, based upon uniquely constructed interview findings, organized along multiple themes: grandmothers' feelings about caregiving, family relationships, the unique problems and contexts of caregiving, coping strategies, the support they receive from others, their values, and perceptions of their role in the family as the hub around which the family revolves.

The richness and diversity of these case-study based interviews is fascinating, and gives the reader much to reflect upon, particularly with regard to the grandmothers' use of their religious and spiritual values in coping with—and indeed, transcending—the demands of raising a grandchild under oftentimes adverse circumstances. Complementing these insightful observations are well-crafted, integrative chapters that richly pull together this very important and significant study's findings, providing us with insights that only a patient and compassionate researcher can appreciate.

Custodial grandparenting presents all caregivers with unique challenges and satisfactions, and *Amazing Grace* paints this picture well, making possible more meaningful research and more effective practice, enabling those who both study and work with grandparent caregivers on a daily basis to more fully understand this complex and ever-evolving role. Its contribution to our knowledge of custodial grandparenting is invaluable.

Bert Hayslip, Ph.D.
*Regents Professor of Psychology*
*University of North Texas*

# Acknowledgments

It is not possible to acknowledge everyone who has influenced the publication of this book. I would like to thank The Duke University Center for the Study of Aging and Human Development for awarding me the grant and providing administrative services to pursue the research. A very special thanks to my mentor, Dr. Linda K. George, Professor of Sociology at Duke University, and Associate Director of the Duke University Center for the Study of Aging and Human Development; Kay Fox, Duke University Center for the Study of Aging and Human Development, for her secretarial support; Dr. Carolyn W. Zhu, Senior Research Associate at the Robert J. Milano Graduate School of Managements and Urban Policy, for her assistance with data analysis; Dr. Martha R. Crowther, Department of Psychology, University of Alabama, for her reading of the original manuscripts; David Landrum, Administrative Assistant in the Department of African American and African Studies at the University of North Carolina at Charlotte, for his organizational support; and his assistant, Ditishia Simpson, student assistant in the Department of African American and African Studies; and Dr. Gregory Davis, Director of Minority Student Services at the University of North Carolina at Charlotte, for his valuable assistance in identifying the appropriate verses of Amazing Grace to be included in this volume.

The research would not have been possible without the support of the Duke University Center for the Study of Aging and Human Development, The National Institutes of Health, National Institute on Aging and

Physiology in Aging Account No. 2T32AG00029, and The National Institute on Aging Account No. R01 AG 15062-03S1. The North Carolina Division on Aging, Durham County Social Services, Durham County Housing Authority, Orange County Housing Authority, African American churches, senior centers, support groups, community nurses, mental health centers, family social workers in public schools, and juvenile detention facilities were among the agencies and organizations involved in this study.

It is important to acknowledge all of the grandparents, their children, and grandchildren whom I have had the good fortune to meet and work with during this research. I have maintained many of these relationships. These grandmothers continue to be "guardian" to their grandchildren and never waver in assuming this responsibility. It is my wish that society will support grandparents as they commit themselves to providing supportive and loving family environments for our young to grow and mature. It is for African American grandmothers and their grandchildren well into the twenty-first century, that I have written this book.

Finally, I want to thank my sons, Jason and Alex, who supported me with grace and understanding as I uprooted them in order to pursue the research fellowship for the study. *May you always be influenced by those whose lives are guided by a sense of purpose and commitment to something bigger than themselves.*

# Introduction

The family and the church have been the most important institutions in African American families and communities since slavery. African American grandmothers have played a pivotal role in both institutions. Their role responsibilities, especially in the extended family context, are broad and elastic. They have performed crucial roles in the care and welfare of grandchildren, great-grandchildren, fictive kin, and others who may or may not be related by birth. In addition to caregiving, African American grandmothers have provided social and emotional support to family members; communicated important social values to offspring; engaged in the birth of babies; worked in the fields along with their husbands; and engaged in important leadership positions in the family, church, and community. From the days of slavery to the present, African American grandmothers have been a major force in the socialization of children and the stabilization of black families. The strength and resilience of African American motherhood is embedded in the ability of these women to withstand the harshness of slavery and oppression, their ability to perform multiple roles, their love of family, and their strong religious beliefs (Ruiz and Carlton-La Ney, 1999; Ruiz, 2000).

In contemporary American society, African American grandmothers have continued their roles as guardians and caregivers while facing new and challenging responsibilities as we approach the twenty-first century. Over the past two decades, there has been an enormous amount of policy and research interest in the roles grandparents play in raising and providing care for their grandchildren. This interest is stimulated by the increasing numbers of grandparent-maintained households. According to the U.S. Bureau of the Census (1997), since 1970, there has been a 77 percent increase in the number of households headed by grandparents. Grandparent-headed households represent all socioeconomic levels and ethnic/racial groups. However, the greatest increase is among African American grandmothers in the role of surrogate parent, where neither parent is present. In spite of the rapid increase, very little research has been devoted to the incidence, prevalence, and problems of grandmother-maintained households within African American communities.

In 1970, 2.2 million or 3.2 percent of American children lived in a home maintained by a grandparent. This number had increased to 3.9 million or 5.5 percent by 1997 (Casper and Bryson 1998; U.S. Bureau of the Census 1998; Velkoff and Lawson 1998). In 1998, this figure had risen to 4 million or 6 percent of all children under 18 (U.S. Bureau of the Census 1998). The greatest increase was among children with only one parent in the household. This pattern, grandchildren living in households maintained by grandparents with only mother present, increased by 118 percent from 1970 to 1997 (Casper and Bryson 1998; U.S. Bureau of the Census 1997). Since 1990, however, the greatest growth has been in the number of grandchildren living with their grandparents only, with neither parent present (Casper and Bryson 1998; U.S. Bureau of the Census 1998).

In their analysis of census data, Taylor, Tucker, Chatters, and Jayakody (1997) observed that white and Hispanic children who lived in their grandparent's home are more likely than black children to have both parents present in the same household (U.S. Bureau of the Census 1992). Data show that 23 percent of white children and 26 percent of Hispanic children who lived in their grandparent's home had both parents present, in comparison to only 2 percent of African American children. Thirty-five percent of African American children who reside with their grandparents live there without either parent present, whereas 21 percent of both white and Hispanic children live with grandparents only. Sixty-three percent of the families headed by white grandparents had both grandparents present, in comparison to 35 percent of families headed by African American grandparents (Taylor, Tucker, Chatters, and Jayakody 1997; U.S. Bureau of the Census 1992). African American children are more likely to live in the home of their grandparents than are whites or Hispanics.

In many ways, the grandmother has been the foundation of black families in the face of difficulties. In spite of the social and economic conditions the black family faced, the black grandmother has been a steady, supporting influence, as well as a connecting link between branches of the extended family. She is viewed as a source of strength and the communicator of family values; providing the religious orientation to family members, and stressing the importance of service to others, racial pride, educational achievement, strong family ties, commitment to children, self-respect, discipline, and hard work. The African American grandmother has socialized her children and grandchildren into values and patterns essential to their survival, growth, and development, providing the foundation for the resilience and endurance of the black family.

Structural changes in society have influenced a rearrangement of nuclear families. Within the last decade, there have been a number of structural changes in African American family life. In his discussion of the diversity in family structure in African American communities, Billingsley (1992) notes that from 1865 to 1965 (the hundred-year period between the end of slavery and until after World War II), the African American family was characterized by a high degree of stability—meaning the central focus of the traditional family was the nuclear family unit consisting of the mother, father, and their children. The decline in two-parent families began after the 1960s, and at a time when it became difficult for black men to maintain decent wages as blue-collar workers in the industrial sector. At the beginning of the 1960s, 78 percent of all black families were headed by married couples, followed by 64 percent in 1970, 48 percent in 1980, and 39 percent in 1990 (Billingsley 1992). Given the social and structural problems faced by African Americans, this downward trend in two-parent families is likely to continue, and grandmother-maintained households will likely increase.

In 1980, Billingsley (1992) noted, for the first time since slavery, a majority of African Americans lived in single-parent families. The nuclear as well as the extended family forms that were adopted after slavery as an adaptive mechanism were in a rapid state of decline (Billingsley 1992). Postindustrialization has resulted in a number of alternative family structures, and grandmothers raising grandchildren alone is among the most obvious. The grandmother-headed family is an adaptive strategy for meeting the basic needs of its members given the situation they face in contemporary society (Billingsley 1992). Technological changes since the 1950s, and more recently the crack-cocaine and HIV/AIDS epidemics and the incarcerations of young mothers have all contributed to the restructuring of the African American family. And, grandmothers have been thrust into unfamiliar and nontraditional caregiving roles that threaten their morale and increase their role confusion (Emick and Hayslip 1996; Hayslip, Shore, Henderson, and Lambert 1998).

Elderly persons raising grandchildren face a number of challenges, such as their own declining health or the need to provide support to the absent parent of a grandchild. Other challenges might include lack of support and respite services, affordable housing, access to medical care, physical and emotional strains, as well as other family problems (Burton and DeVries 1993; Kelly 1993; Minkler and Roe 1993; Minkler and Roe 1996). Some may not have the financial resources to raise another family, and may need to deplete their savings to support their grandchildren. Others do not welcome the role of grandparenthood, especially in the case of young grandmothers who experience role conflict between work and caregiving (Burton and DeVries 1993).

This volume highlights the increase in grandparent caregivers over the past thirty years, with specific emphasis on role responsibilities and contemporary challenges for the grandmothers. The book begins with the historical family roles of older African American women, provides related research, describes the methodology, continues with quantitative and qualitative analyses, and ends with the direction of future research.

Chapter 1 provides an overview of the literature on the impact of older women on the black family. Role comparisons are identified in Africa, during slavery, and after the Civil War. Their roles as teachers, spiritual leaders, and conveyers of traditional values are discussed. Chapter 2 provides a literature review of grandparent caregivers. Literature includes the census data describing the increase in grandparent caregiving; reasons for caregiving; the problems and burdens associated with custodial caregiving; the impact of drugs, incarcerations, and AIDS on caregiving; as well as the health and social consequences of long-term caregiving. Chapter 3 describes the methodological procedures. Both quantitative and qualitative methods were used to collect and analyze data. The next three chapters cover the quantitative analysis of the study: Chapter 4 includes the social and demographic characteristics of the sample; Chapter 5 provides an analysis of life satisfaction and custodial caregiving; and Chapter 6 describes the relationship between depression, social factors, and custodial caregiving. Chapter 7 provides a qualitative analysis of some of the dominant themes resulting from the reaseach. These include family structure and relationships, attitudes about caregiving, assumption of the caregiver role, grandmothers' perceptions of social problems, unusual circumstances of caregiving, self-definitions from grandmothers, value orientation, and functions associated with caregiving. The Conclusion provides a brief summary and some recommendations for future research.

# Slavery, Family, and Religion: The Traditional Roles of Older African American Women in the Antebellum South during the Nineteenth Century

They were full of sturdiness and singing.

*—Dorothy Sterling*

Religion and the importance of family are two of the strongest and most meaningful traditions in the lives of African Americans, and grandmothers have performed important helping roles in both institutions. From their early beginnings in this country to the present, African American grandmothers have been instrumental in their roles as caregivers and nurturers within extended family networks. Traditional caregiving roles have included caring for children, grandchildren, great-grandchildren, nieces, nephews, and a number of other relatives and nonrelatives. Older African American women, particularly grandmothers, set the standards for suitable behavior. It is often the grandmothers who provide direction and advice on education, sexual conduct, self-respect, religious practices, love, and other important social values. Their position as caregivers and advisors is matched by their role as providers of social and emotional support to family members. African American grandmothers are appropriately described by E. Franklin Frazier (1939) as the *guardian[s] of the generations*.

Viewed as powerful, capable, effective and resourceful, African American grandmothers are significant figures in the endurance and subsistence of the black family. Their roles as socializers of young children and stabilizers of families must not be understated. The strength and resilience of black grand-motherhood is firmly established in her ability to withstand the brutality of slavery and oppression, her love of family, her strong religious values, and her ability to carry out complicated role responsibilities. Therefore, as we begin a new century, it seems appropriate and timely that we reflect on the hopes and dreams of African American grandmothers, who have served as health care providers, faith healers, nurturers, and guardians. In an effort to captivate the nature of the grandmother role during the nineteenth century, a number of role positions will be discussed and analyzed with reference to her African heritage and her slave experience in America. As a survivor herself and a stabilizer for the family and community, the grandmother role will be discussed within the context of the African family, her own character, the slave community, and the slave family.

## THE AFRICAN FAMILY

Historians report that the first Africans that arrived in Jamestown, Virginia, in 1619, "represented everything African," although most were the descendants of the people of the West African gold and ivory coasts (Du Bois 1962, 3). The approximately 10 million Africans transported from Africa to the Americas between the fifteenth and nineteenth centuries came from many tribes: "the Bantu tribes from Sierra Leone to South Africa; the Sudanese from the Atlantic to the Valley of the Nile, the Nilotic Negroes, and the black and brown Hamites associated with Egypt, the tribes of the great lakes; and the Pygmies and the Hottentots" (Du Bois 1962, 3). The majority of Africans who eventually ended up in the United States did so by way of the West Indies. They brought with them such African traditions as their rhythmic song, traces of their art, and tribal customs (Du Bois 1962). They also brought their spiritual beliefs and their close family ties.

The family unit in precolonial African society was highly structured, rigidly patriarchal, and very important (Blassingame 1972). Significance was placed on the clear-cut roles of both men and women. In his work, *The Negro in the Making of America,* Benjamin Quarles (1964) describes the traditional West African family as kinship groupings numbering in the hundreds. The extended family network was characterized by close kinship ties and political, economic, and social organization. Kinship groups lived in a defined geographical area and felt responsible to support and take care of each other. The dominant figure in the extended family community was the patriarch who had a number of political, social, and economic functions; acting as peacemaker, judge, administrator, and keeper of the purse. Other functions of the patriarch were making hoes, shovels, spears, shields, and swords (Blassingame 1972). Women, in the patriarchal family unit, were uncommonly graceful, alert, modest, bashful, and chaste. They too performed important roles in the patriarchal family structure. "Regardless of the meaningful roles of women in precolonial Africa," however, "the authority pattern was patriarchal" (Staples 1976, 115). Women's roles included weaving calico cloth and making clothing and earthenware. They also served as warriors and did the marketing. The care and training of children was primarily the responsibility of women. And, as a result, deep bonds of affection developed between mothers and their children.

The kinship groups were organized around very defined relationships between children and adults, and such relationships became an instrumental part of the African tradition regarding adult–child interactions. And, according to Gutman (1976), authority over children was vested in parents, but monitored by grandparents who maintained "a relationship of friendly familiarity and almost social equity" with children (199). As reported by Pollard (1981), the elderly in African cultures had "special roles and functions that continued in slavery" (228). They were instrumental in connecting the past to the present, in that they were storytellers to young children and communicators of important religious values. Elderly men and women were considered conveyors of the culture.

The roles and functions of elderly Africans elevated them to high positions of honor in extended family networks and in the community. Pollard (1981) writes that the elderly "maintained a continuous engagement with society through the maintenance of respected and powerful positions in the social structure of their respective communities" (228). The notability of the grandmother in American slavery was consistent with her prominence in the African society, although her role expectations, due to the demands of slavery, were different. Ladner (1971) notes that the roles of women in precolonial Africa were important, but different from their roles in American society.

## THE ROLE AND CHARACTER OF GRANDMOTHERS
## DURING SLAVERY

The strong character of African American grandmothers and the significance of their roles are undisputed by the literature. "Perhaps even higher than strength and art loom human sympathy and sacrifice as characteristic of Negro womanhood," Du Bois notes in his appraisal of black womanhood (1975, 171). Although she occupied a number of significant roles, "the most visible portrait of the black grandmother in all the literature is one of action, involvement, hope, and dignity" (Hill-Lubin 1991, 174). The grandmother roles were broad and expansive and included far more than just caring for their grandchildren. In her analysis of the historical roles of grandmothers in three literary works, Hill-Lubin (1991) identifies three categories of grandmother functions. These being (1) "preserver of the African extended family," (2) "repository and distributor of the family history, wisdom, and black lore," and (3) "retainer and communicator of values and ideals that support and enhance her humanity, her family, and her community" (174). Here one can see the grandmother as the influence on keeping the family intact, communicating family history, and socializing family members into accepting important cultural values.

In addition to their voluntary role as keeper and helper to their families, older women were forced to accept total responsibility for their families in many cases; placing undo hardship on women to work in the fields and take care of their own children as well as the master's children and his family. "Negro women could be put to tasks, particularly work in the fields, that would not be expected of white women" (Quarles 1964, 37). Slave women were compelled to assume responsibility for their families that "men assumed in the white world" (Ladner 1971, 17). The "crushing weight of slavery fell on black women" (Du Bois 1975, 179).

In an effort to present the character, strength, burdens and values of black women during the later nineteenth and early twentieth centuries, Du Bois (1975) writes,

As I look about me today in this veiled world of mine, despite the noisier and more spectacular advance of my brothers, I instinctively feel and know that it is the five million women of my race who really count. Black women (and women whose grandmothers were black) are today furnishing our teachers; they are the main pillars of those social settlements which we call churches; and they have with small doubt raised three-fourths of our church property. If we have today, as seems likely, over a billion dollars of accumulated goods, who shall say how much of it has been wrung from the hearts of servant girls and washerwomen and women toilers in the fields? As makers of two million homes, these women are today seeking marvelous ways to show forth our strength and beauty and our conception of the truth. (179)

In this passage, one sees an evolution of roles from the antebellum to the postbellum era. Du Bois shows how the strength and character of grandmothers are displayed through their roles as teachers, spiritual leaders, and wealth builders. As teachers and spiritual leaders, grandmothers, through storytelling, taught survival techniques as well as ways to progress as a race and live fully functioning lives. They socialized their children and grandchildren in the understanding and knowledge of delivering babies and home remedies for illnesses. "In many ways, the black woman is the carrier of culture because it has been she who has epitomized what it meant to be black, oppressed . . . it was she who survived in a country where survival was not always considered possible" (Ladner 1971, 287). Because of the grandmother's skills and wisdom, she "occupies a special place and is viewed on a higher plane than others by both the black and white communities" (Hill-Lubin 1991, 176). She had "keen insights into human relations," and "proficiency in home and people management" (Hill-Lubin, 177).

The unique aspect of the grandmother character is her insistence on protecting her children and grandchildren and providing for her family. There are numerous examples in the literature where grandmothers exemplify courage, strength, and determination to protect their young from life's harsh realities. African American grandmothers, through all of their struggles, "possess a quiet kind of dignity, matched with strength, courage, and determination that often make them appear invincible" (Hill-Lubin 1991, 179). And, finally, the character of grandmothers is esteemed once again, when Du Bois says, "I most sincerely doubt if any other race of women could have brought its fineness up through so devilish a fire" (1997, 171).

## ROLES OF GRANDMOTHERS IN THE COMMUNITY OF SLAVES

It was during the nineteenth century that the strong roles of black women emerged (Staples 1976). However, except for a few slave narratives such as those by Frederick Douglass and Gustavus Vassa (Olaudah Equiano), not much literature reflects the roles of grandparents prior to the Civil War. It is not clear whether this is a function of different conceptual definitions of mother and grandmother within the same household, or whether the grandmother role was more subdued during slavery. Perhaps, the grandmother role during early American slavery was more similar to her role in the African culture—that of an overseer. Or perhaps the duality of the mother and grandmother roles in the lives of the child made clear-cut role distinctions difficult for early writers and observers. The conceptual definitions between mother and grandmother during slavery may be somewhat unclear, but it is clear that the roles of older women during slavery made it possible for the system to exist and flourish. Although sketchy, the literature on the roles of grandmothers during slavery is consistent in representing their strength, devotion, and love for their families.

Notable among the many characteristics of the African American family during slavery are the roles of older women. Powdermaker (1969) found that the typical household consisted of grandparents, nieces, nephews, adopted children, and others who were not related even by adoption. Older women, usually grandmothers, gave the family its unity, cohesion, perceptiveness, wisdom, and sense of purpose. In his book, *The Negro in the Unites States* (1957), E. Franklin Frazier notes that African American grandmothers played important roles in the survival of the family. He describes the importance of grandmothers in the following passage:

The Negro grandmother's importance is due to the fact not only that she has been the "oldest head" in a maternal family organization but also to her position as "granny" or midwife among a simple peasant folk. As the repository of folk wisdom concerning the inscrutable ways of nature, the grandmother has been depended upon by mothers to ease the pains of childbirth and ward off the danger of ill luck. Children acknowledge their indebtedness to her for assuring them, during the crisis of birth, a safe entrance into the world. Even grown men and women refer to her as a second mother and sometimes show the same deference and respect for her that they accord their own mothers. (117)

The grandmother's presence, influence, authority, and prestige in the black family structure is an established fact. Powdermaker (1969) notes that grandmothers were present in many households, and were likely to have more influence than mothers in the child's life, although the biological mother maintained the authority. Frequently, the grandmothers were left at home when the mother went to work. However, because of early marriages, the grandmother was often young enough for strenuous labor. When an elderly women is head of a household that includes married daughters, says Powdermaker (1969), she carries authority with the children, and even when her position is less dominant, she is likely to take over responsibility for their welfare and behavior. Most women were as eager for grandchildren as for children, and often for the same reasons. "Grandparents loomed large in the life of the slave child—they frequently prepared tidbits for the children, and grandfathers often told them stories about their lives in Africa" (Blassingame 1972, 95).

Grandmothers also fulfilled vital roles in the plantation economy during slavery. As a result of their many roles, grandmothers were valued and respected highly by both fellow slaves and masters alike. The loyalty, devotion, and reverence accorded the grandmothers by extended family and the master and his family was surpassed by that of any other family member. Frazier (1939) writes that the grandmother "keeps secrets and was seen as loyal and affectionate by the master, and the defender of the family honor" (114). She "possessed a tenacity of spirit, a gift of endurance, a steadfastness of aspiration that helped a whole population to survive" (Sterling 1984, 39). She became an irreplaceable member in the family because of her ability to perform a number of different economic and social roles.

Women were both the center of a labor force and the generator of wealth. A woman's value was measured by the number of children she had, and even more if the children were "strong and muley." Sterling found that in the decades before the Civil War, a mother's child was worth $100 at birth, and $500 at the age of five. The well, young, and judicious "breed women" had property value (Sterling 1984, 31). With regard to race and gender, African American women have performed more multifaceted roles than any other group. Regardless of the quantity of work she performed outside the home, however, she always returned to her cabin and took care of her traditional roles as wife and mother.

However, when slaves became too old or too frail to perform agricultural duties, they were assigned to household responsibilities. These might include taking care of the babies, disciplining the children, nursing the sick, sewing and knitting, cooking, caring for farm animals, and polishing and repairing tools (Pollard 1981). Other roles might include advisor, authority on first babies, wet nurse, and confidant. In cases where mothers and children were separated, the children were also raised by their grandmothers or older women in the slave community who were too old to work (Hill-Lubin 1991, 177).

## THE ROLE OF GRANDMOTHERS IN STRENGTHENING FAMILY TIES

The slave family was one of the most important survival mechanisms for the slave, although "it had no legal existence" (Blassingame 1972, 78). The family was a source of social and emotional support, and although frequently separated, the family cohesion made it possible for the slaves to survive. The family provided love, companionship, a common understanding of suffering, and lessons on avoiding punishment and cooperating with other slaves. Although difficult, the family was important in maintaining self-esteem. "The family was largely responsible for the slave's survival on the plantation without becoming totally dependent on, and submissive to, his master" (Blassingame 1972, 78–79). Family ties existed and kept families connected spiritually, emotionally, and socially. The "family ties came to mean chiefly the ties that bound women to children and later grandchildren" (Powdermaker 1969, 144). The immediate family and the enlarged kinship groups were among the central binding institutions within slave communities (Gutman 1976). And, in spite of its harshness, "slavery did not destroy the slaves' capacity to adapt and sustain the vital familial and kin associations and beliefs that served as the underpinning of a developing Afro-American culture" (Gutman 1976, 465).

### After Emancipation

The slave family entered the post–Civil War era with a markedly established foundation. Despite many historical misconceptions, "the slaves created impressive norms of family life, including as much of a nuclear family norm as conditions permitted" (Genovese 1976, 453). Genovese writes that families with strong needs for stability established behavior forms in freedom that served and maintained their own self-interest as well as the needs and interests of the dominant society. The bonds between husbands and wives, parents and children, nieces and nephews, aunts and uncles, and especially brothers and sisters were clear. And the strength of family ties was seen more vividly in reactions to separations prior to emancipation.

After the Civil War, much of the family life of the slave existed around the grandmother. Grandmothers provided cohesion for the family by offering both material and spiritual support to their children and grandchildren. It was often the grandmother who "kept the generations together" (Frazier 1939, 116), while the mothers worked and many fathers went out to find their lost children and wives. It was the grandmother says Frazier, who held the generations together when fathers and even mothers abandoned their offspring. Grandmothers assumed enormous responsibility for the care and welfare of their families and displayed much love and devotion. The following passage, taken from Frazier's 1939 work, depicts the energy, courage, and devotion of a 70-year-old grandmother:

During the Civil War, an old slave and his wife attempted to escape from a plantation near Savannah, but were caught and returned to their master. While the old man was receiving five hundred lashes as punishment, his wife collected his children and grandchildren, to the number of twenty-two, in a neighboring marsh, preparatory to another attempt that night. They found a flatboat which had been rejected as unseaworthy, got on board—still under the woman's orders—drifted forty miles down the river to the lines of the Union army. An officer who was on board the gunboat that picked them up said that "when the 'flat' touched the side of the vessel, the grandmother rose to her full height with her grandchild in her arms, and said only "My God! Are we free?" (114)

The courage exhibited in that passage represents the commitment grandmothers have for their families. Grandmothers take pride in carrying a heavy burden without letting the world know. They work diligently and suffer silently and take pride in doing what is necessary to support their families. In her twentieth-century appraisal of African American women, bell hooks (1981) writes that the portrayals of black women that are viewed as positive are often those that depict her as a long-suffering, religious, maternal woman whose most persistent characteristic is her self-sacrificing and self-denial for those she loves.

Frazier (1957) writes that during the later nineteenth and early twentieth centuries, the mother-headed family functioned like an organization in the rural South. As has been noted, during slavery, the mother was the most reliable individual in the family; however, after emancipation, the matri-centric family grew into a type of so-called matriarchy "in which the grandmother was the dominant figure" (Frazier 1957, 320). Because of her age and experience, the grandmother has authority over the daughter and her children and assumes responsibility for their welfare. The "matriarchal" family structure consisted of an extended family network, including several generations of nieces, nephews, and adopted children. As an extension of her duties from slavery, the grandmother was a storehouse of folk wisdom and was called upon during the major crises in life. Her exceptional wisdom and authority, however, rested in her knowledge of childbirth and related matters.

## The Spiritual and Leadership Roles of African American Grandmothers

The traditional folk culture for African Americans was religion and their relationship to the church. The church has been of particular importance in rural Southern communities. The religious way of life for African Americans in the South was inseparable from the community. During the nineteenth and early twenty-first centuries, the church was the community. As E. Franklin Frazier contends, "a particular church defined the limits of the communal life. It has been in the church that the Negro has found a meaning for his existence, and it was the church that enlisted his deepest loyalties" (Frazier 1957, 117). The church, along with its spiritual benefits, has also been a source of social control. Traditionally, it has been older African American women, particularly grandmothers, who have enforced normative behavior, good moral conduct, and spiritual teachings to members of the black family. In light of the role older women play in the survival and strength of black American families, this chapter will emphasize (1) the historical roles of older African American women and religion during slavery, (2) grandmothers as spiritual leaders and bearers of black culture, (3) roles of grandmothers in the slave community, and (4) contemporary views on religion and grandparenthood.

The strong historical roles of older African women in the church and family are well known, but not well documented. Religion is central to the experiences of African American families and grandmothers have performed major functions in both institutions. Both the family and religion were significant stabilizing factors for enslaved Africans in the antebellum South. Within the family, the grandmother functions as the preserver of the extended family, and communicator of history and social values. Within both the church and family, she functions as teacher and spiritual leader. Expressing spirituality is a regular and significant part of the grandmother's interaction with others. African American grandmothers have not only maintained the integrity of the extended family network, but also a creative spirit. The role of God in the lives of older women is unquestioned. Religion was the only sure hope for a people whose experiences were extremely destitute. Religious beliefs and practices among older women encompass a distinct tradition within the experiences of blacks in this country.

## The Roles of Older Women and Religion

Religion, and older women's leadership roles in it, was a powerful source of communal life socially, culturally and economically within the slave community. Slaves prayed for freedom and prayer was also used to "ensure bountiful crops" (Close 1998, 65). Often, a strong belief in God was consistent with all aspects of social life, and particularly important in maintaining good mental health. During slavery, faith in God is what made life bearable. "Faith in God and commitment to service was insepara-ble" (Guthrie 1995, 165). Service to others is important to African Ameri-cans, particularly older women. Commitment to service gives meaning to their lives and serves as the basis for good psychological health. Spiritual-ity and the church are essential life features for African Americans in main-taining good mental health and community relationships, as well as combating racial discrimination and oppression. The spirituality of older African American women has empowered them to make significant progress in the struggles against injustice and inequality in America.

Although older African American women have traditionally been the foundation of the church, they have not played significant leadership roles (Hayes 1995) within this institution. African American churches are heav-ily female, and Guthrie (1995) estimates that women constitute approxi-mately 75 percent of the membership. Women have traditionally been the backbone of the African American church as well as the African American family. The programmatic and economic foundation of the black church is largely due to the involvement and supportive leadership roles of older women. They built and maintained the churches wherein they have asserted their economic and structural importance (Guthrie 1995). African American women have been involved in all aspects of community life, organization, and service during slavery and after emancipation.

In addition to their roles as a spiritual leader, teacher, and fighter for social causes, older grandmothers disciplined the children and took care of the babies while parents worked in the fields. In this position, they were instrumental in a number of ways. They became spiritual leaders for the children by teaching them the power of God and how to pray. They also taught them hymns and Negro spirituals while in their care. "The slave children believed their grandmothers' prayers would free them from slav-ery" (Close 1998, 70). Other important values were taught, including respect for others and moral behavior.

African American women like Sojourner Truth, Ida B. Wells, and count-less others displayed spiritual faith and strength that led them to stand up for the rights of women and blacks in general. Strong African American mothers and grandmothers did not allow the "limitations of their circum-stances to shape their perspective on life" writes Diana Hayes in *Hagar's Daughters* (1995, 3). Grandmothers believed in freedom and the "eventual triumph of good over evil" and "found solace in the spirit to remain sane" (Wade–Gayles and Finch 1995, 81). The slaves used the phrase "no shack-les on the souls" to symbolize the power of the human spirit to move to new heights. African American grandmothers have been described by Hayes as the "keepers of the faith, bearers of the culture, and fanners of the flame" (1995, 16). In short, they possess the strength and tenacity that has enabled succeeding generations to survive as well as thrive.

## Grandmothers as Spiritual Leaders and Bearers of the Black Culture

Although historically the church leaders have been primarily men, the spiritual teachers and the "conveyers of spiritual possession and the Christian religion of the slave community" have been primarily older women (Close 1998, 69). It was often the grandparent, the grandmother in particular, from whom children learned their religious beliefs. The aged were well respected by youth during slavery, not only for their age and wisdom, but also for their position as religious leaders in the community. Grandmothers played important roles in maintaining moral behavior and "sustaining the religious lives of families in enslaved communities" by influencing religious practices in these communities (Close 1998, 63). Older women demonstrated control over others by reminding them of their propensity to backslide, as the minister often does. Religious testimony was lead by older women, and even today is still mostly influenced by older women in African American churches. During slavery, older women were clearly the leaders in the practice and teaching of religion, and this influence has continued through the post–Civil Rights era.

In the community of slaves, older women exercised much power and control, not only in the family, but also in the church and the community at large. Older women were the practitioners and leaders of much of the spirit possession in the religion of the slave community says Creel (1988). Creel notes that they were often the first members of the slave community to shout and praise God. "The grandmother was a powerful Christian woman, who loved to sing and shout" (Close 1998, 69). There was a tendency for older black women to practice their religion more openly than men. The religious practices of the grandmother served to keep the slave community hopeful and alive. Religious leadership provided elderly women with a feeling of belonging. This resulted in a high degree of love and respect for elderly African Americans, particularly the grandmother, that transcended the slave era. Even after emancipation, religious practices were important in the lives of African Americans (Gilkes 1993).

## Reverence and Support for Older Slaves

During slavery, the elderly were treated with high respect by the slave community. Genovese (1976) notes that slaves, including the children, treated them with respect and deference that lessened humiliations and disrespect placed on them by condescending whites. Older persons in the African American family have traditionally been treated as if they are needed. In cases where older members were treated with "indifference or hostility others in the community would step in and assume responsibility" (Genovese 1976, 522). After emancipation, the older slaves were confident that they would be taken care of by family, friends, and the black community.

The dignity and respect received by grandparents eminated from many sources, however, their knowledge of folk medicine "gave old folks a special role that made them feel especially useful and respected . . . bringing them consideration born of religious sanctions as well as physical service" (Genovese 1976, 523). In his discussion of the reverence accorded to grandmothers, Frazier (1939) notes that their "superior wisdom and authority are recognized chiefly in matters concerning childbirth," although her spiritual knowledge plays a significant role in her influence over the family and in the community (320). Within the slave community, she was considered the midwife who provided knowledge to young mothers about babies and took care of them during childbirth.

Health care was an important role for older women. Taking care of the sick and delivering babies brought esteem, wisdom, and prestige to the roles of older women. They took pride in teaching these skills to their children and grandchildren. They also felt proud of their own knowledge and wisdom. Older slaves exemplified a high degree of emotional and physical security. The old folks' ability to live decently and with self-respect depended primarily on the support of their young slaves (Genovese 1976, xx).

### From Slavery to the Present: Contemporary Views on Spirituality and Grandmotherhood

The spiritual and religious teachings of older African Americans, particularly the grandmother, were broad and expansive, and included more than just the teaching of the scriptures and how to pray. Religion served as an integral part of their daily lives. The grandmother's teachings included important social and spiritual values such as advice on how to live a good life, the importance of giving back to the community, the need for women to be able to take care of themselves with the help of God, self-respect, and the importance of serving God. "The Bible says, 'to whom much is given, much is required,' " they would say.

Grandmothers stressed the role of God in our everyday lives. A common saying in African American communities is "the Lord never gives you more than you can handle" and "the Lord helps those who help themselves." Grandmothers felt that no burden was too heavy and that if you do your part, God will do the rest. A strong faith is an African American legacy from grandmothers. It has been the grandmother who provides spiritual wisdom, a strong faith in God, hope, and encouragement. They are truly leaders in the family, church, and the community. African American grandmothers have many honorable characteristics, but perhaps E. Franklin Frazier said it best in 1939, when he stated that African American grandmothers are guardians of the generations.

## CONCLUSION

Often viewed as strong and resourceful, African American grandmothers have performed crucial roles for the survival and stability of the black family. Even today, as grandmothers have migrated to urban centers, they have continued to care for their grandchildren in spite of economic and social demands such as teen pregnancy, AIDS, drug abuse, and the incarceration of their children. The words of E. Franklin Frazier are as true today as they were approximately seventy years ago when he said, "the Negro grandmother has not ceased to watch over the destiny of the Negro families as they have moved in ever-increasing numbers to the cities" (1939, 223). The African American grandmother continues to exercise authority over family members in extended households and assumes responsibility for their welfare. She continues to maintain superior wisdom and is depended upon during the major and minor crises of life. Even where there is no crisis, the grandmother still serves in the capacity of queen as well as king. As we enter the twenty-first century, African American grandmothers still remain "guardians of the generations," as well as conveyers of black culture, spiritual leaders, and nurturers. Du Bois (1975) took pride in writing about the reverence and esteem he held for black women:

No other women on earth could have emerged from the hell of force and temptation which once engulfed and still surrounds black women in American with half the modesty and womanliness that they retain. I have always felt like bowing myself before them in all abasement, searching to bring some tribute to these long-suffering victims, these burdened sisters of mine, whom the world, the wise, white world, loves to affront and ridicule and wantonly to insult. I have known and seen and lived beside them, but none have I known more sweetly feminine, more unswervingly loyal, more desperately earnest, and more instinctively pure in body and in soul than the daughters of my black mothers. This then—a little thing—to their memory and inspiration. (186)

# 2

# Related Research: Grandparent Caregiving

Changing demographic and socioeconomic trends have drastically influenced the structure of African American families (Billingsley 1992). The early 1990s brought increased attention to the number of grandchildren living in grandparent-maintained households; however, census data document a trend beginning as early as the 1970s. According to the U.S. Census Bureau reports (1992), the number of children under 18 living in grandparent-maintained households increased from 2.2 million in 1970, to 2.3 million in 1980, to 3.3 million in 1992. In 1970, slightly more than 3 percent of all children under 18 were living in a home maintained by a grandparent. This number had increased to almost 5 percent by 1992. Recent research and census data show that this trend has continued. In 1997, for example, 3.9 million children lived in a home maintained by a grandparent; constituting 5.5 percent of all children less than 18 years old (Bryson and Casper 1999).

In addition to these general trends, significant increases have occurred in the number of children living with grandparents and only one or no biological parent. Between 1970 and 1992, the greatest increase was among grandchildren living with grandparents and only one parent (Bryson and Casper 1999). However, between 1992 and 1997, the greatest increase occurred among grandchildren living with grandparents only and no biological parent. In 1997, about 4.7 million grandparents were living with their grandchildren, consisting of 2.9 million grandmothers compared with 1.7 million grandfathers (Bryson and Casper 1999).

Maximiliane Szinovacz (1998), in an analysis of the National Survey of Families and Household (NSFA) data, found higher prevalence rates than those found in the U.S. Census. In Wave 2 of the NSFH data, conducted between 1992 and 1994 ($n = 10,008$), she found that 26 percent of African American and approximately 23 percent of Hispanic grandmothers lived in households with grandparents, in comparison to 7 percent of white grandmothers and 4 percent of white grandfathers. These results show that more than 25 percent of African American grandmothers and 13 percent of white grandmothers were custodial grandmothers at some time during their lives (Szinovacz 1998). African Americans were more likely to be grandparent caregivers than other races. A general conclusion in demographic studies (Fuller-Thomson, Minkler, and Driver 1997; Szinovacz 1998) is that custodial caregiving among grandmothers is prevalent in the population and involves long-term commitment.

A number of reasons might explain the high number of grandmother caregivers compared with grandfathers: (1) the high mortality rate among men; (2) the less likelihood of women to remarry after the death of a spouse; (3) the increased poverty associated with being an older single woman, and the likelihood that older women will live with children because of financial reasons; (4) the influence of societal norms governing caregiving responsibilities; and (5) the impact of marital status—divorced or never married (Bryson and Casper 1999).

Grandmothers often assume care of their grandchildren as a result of family crisis such as drug use among parents, unemployment, teen pregnancy, divorce, abuse and neglect, abandonment, and death of a parent (Billingsley 1992; Burton 1992; Minkler, Roe, and Price 1992). They also assume care of their grandchildren because of some of the more recent societal problems such as AIDS (Honey 1988; LeBlanc, London, and Aneshensel 1997) and incarceration of the parents of the grandchildren (Barnhill 1996; Dressel and Barnhill 1994). In spite of the growing interest among researchers, policy makers, and practitioners, there is currently very little empirical research on the demographic, social, and health factors influencing caregiving in intergenerational households. This research is designed to address some of these concerns.

## AFRICAN AMERICAN GRANDMOTHERS: RAISING A SECOND GENERATION

In African American families, it is not uncommon for grandparents to assume responsibility for a grandchild, great-grandchild, niece, or nephew when a parent is no longer able or willing to care for their children. The high proportion of African American children living with grandparents, grandmothers in particular, reflects a continuing pattern of coresidence and shared caregiving in African American families (Roe, Minkler, and

Barnwell 1994; Stack 1974; Wilson 1986). Over the past two decades, the crack-cocaine epidemic, AIDS, and the incarcerations of the grandchildren's parents, have contributed to the dramatic increase in the prevalence of surrogate parenting by African American grandmothers. It is this unprecedented proliferation of grandmothers who are caring for large numbers of grandchildren that has received the nation's attention.

Many of these grandmothers are elderly, and encounter a number of challenges. Their own failing health, or the need to provide support to the absent parent of the grandchild, often present problems. Other challenges might include lack of support, respite care, affordable housing, and access to good medical care; psychological issues; and other family problems that put a strain on her ability to care for the grandchildren (Burton and DeVries 1993; Kelley 1993; Minkler and Roe 1993; Minkler and Roe 1996). Some grandparents may not have the financial resources to take care of their grandchildren and must return to work or use their savings to support them, while others are simply not comfortable in the role of grandparenthood, particularly young grandmothers who experience role conflict between work and caregiving (Burton and DeVries 1993). These challenges are intensified by the conditions of some grandmothers who dwell in communities infested with crime, poverty, disorganization, and the sale and use of crack cocaine.

## AFRICAN AMERICAN GRANDMOTHERS: CARING FOR GRANDCHILDREN AFFECTED BY THE CRACK-COCAINE EPIDEMIC

The crack-cocaine epidemic has serious consequences for African American families and communities (Seamon 1992). A number of studies have cited the consequences of the crack-cocaine epidemic on African American grandmothers who are caring for their grandchildren (Burton 1992; Minkler, Roe, and Robertson-Beckley 1994; Roe, Minkler, and Barnwell 1994; Seamon 1992). Substance abuse is the most common reason for the increase in the number of children living with grandparents (Minkler, Roe, and Robert-Beckley, 1994), although not much is known about how this problem affects the well-being of the grandchildren and the grandmother caregiver. Caring for grandchildren in the midst of the drug epidemic may result in emotional problems and hardships for the grandmother as well as for grandchildren whose parents are actively involved with drugs.

In a 1992 Special Committee on Aging report, "Grandparents as Parents: Raising a Second Generation," Dr. Evelyn Davis, Director of Developmental Pediatrics at Harlem Hospital Center, studied 175 African American children under 6 years old, who were prenatally exposed to crack cocaine and other drugs. She testified that approximately 40 percent of all children referred to her were cared for by grandparents. In her statement, she emphasized the problems grandparents faced in trying to care for their drug-exposed grandchildren with unique behavioral and developmental problems. Davis found that the grandchildren suffered from a number of abnormalities resulting from the mothers' drug use. Among these were premature births (36 percent), language delay (90 percent), fine motor delay (63 percent), gross motor delay (37 percent), delay in social skills (50 percent), hyperactivity (39 percent), neurological problems requiring treatment (30 percent), retardation and autism (8 percent), cerebral palsy (8 percent), and sleep problems (50 percent). A majority of the children had problems with impulsive behavior, and the inability to learn from past mistakes.

New problems for African American grandmothers present challenging role responsibilities. Many welcome the grandparent role, whereas others see it as a burden (Burton and DeVries 1993; Minkler and Roe 1993, 1996). In their study of surrogate parenting, Burton and DeVries (1993) reported that African American grandparents, for the most part, view their role as necessary for the survival of the family. This role assumption reflects the strengths of grandmothers and the resiliency and adaptability of African American families (Billingsley 1992). It is common in African American families for grandmothers to routinely put the needs of their family above their own. Satisfying the needs of their family is synonymous with satisfying their own needs. In fact, the needs of their family are intricately connected to their own identity. The strength and survival of African American families is dependent on the commitment and unselfish acts of grandmothers.

Although grandmothers love their grandchildren and are committed to caring for them, their grandparenting roles may not always be gratifying (Burton and DeVries 1993). Some custodial grandmothers expressed dismay because there were so many things they had to deal with in providing care for their grandchildren. Concerns involved the permanence of childcare, school, social, and physical activities. Other problems included multiple child care responsibilities resulting in stress, job-related conflicts for grandmothers who were working, and limited time for themselves (Burton and DeVries 1993). The child care demands placed on African American grandmothers have left many of them socially isolated and lacking in social support.

### The Impact of Incarcerations on African American Grandmother Caregivers

There has been a dramatic increase in the rate of incarcerations among women over the past decade. Incarcerations among women have increased by 202 percent over the last ten years (Dressel and Barnhill 1994). Approximately fifty thousand women are in state and federal prisons, and some thirty-nine thousand more are in jails. Two-thirds of these women have children under the age of 18 and approximately 53 percent of these children live with their grandparents while their mother is in prison. In most cases, the grandmother is the primary caregiver. Approximately thirty-two thousand older women are primary caregivers for their grandchildren whose mothers are incarcerated (Dressel and Barnhill 1994). It is estimated that seventy-five thousand grandmothers will be faced with the increasing incidence of incarcerations of their grandchildren's mothers before the century's end (Barnhill 1996). African American grandmothers are increasingly called upon to act as surrogate parents for their grandchildren whose mothers are incarcerated or otherwise incapacitated because of drug abuse (Barnhill 1996; Dressel and Barnhill 1994).

The increasing prevalence of incarcerations among young African American mothers creates additional problems for poor and elderly African American grandmothers who are living on fixed incomes, and who may have other child care or kin care responsibilities. In their 1994 case study, Dressel and Barnhill found that this particular population of grandmothers had material needs in almost all basic aspects of life. They also found that the grandmothers' psychological needs focused on respite from and validation for their family work, desire for a better relationship with the incarcerated daughter, and ways to deal with the emotional needs of grandchildren and their behavioral disruptions at home and school (1994). The authors reported that many problems for the grandmother are grandchildren centered around transition periods, such as the daughter's arrest, her conviction, and her release after many years. These transitions may present critical problems in family relationships between the daughter and the grandmother caregiver.

The increase in incarcerations of young mothers is serious and requires attention from social scientists as well as the African American community. Little or no empirical research has been done on the burden on African American grandmothers who must take care of the imprisoned daughter's children. Although the numbers are not very large, they are increasing rapidly (Dressel and Barnhill 1994). We need to know more about the particular needs and problems of this population of grandmother caregivers, and assess some similarities and differences to other groups.

## Consequences of Custodial Parenting among African American Grandmothers

Problems associated with custodial caregiving cause considerable stress for grandmothers. Linda Burton (1992), in her study of grandmothers caring for children affected by the crack-cocaine epidemic, found that 86 percent of the sample felt depressed or anxious most of the time. Similarly, Evelyn Davis (1992) found that grandmothers reported feeling overwhelmed by the many clinic visits required by their grandchildren.

Retarded or autistic children are often involved in special programs requiring the weekly involvement of the primary caregiver. Because of their involvement with the grandchildren, grandmothers often neglect their own social, emotional, and physical needs (Davis 1992). In their analysis of instrumental and emotional support among seventy-one African American grandmothers raising grandchildren as a consequence of the crack-cocaine epidemic, Minkler, Roe, and Robertson-Beckley (1994) found that many women reported decreased contact with family and friends and a decline in marital satisfaction. Others reported that providing care for grandchildren was complicated because they had not finished rearing their own children. The importance of African American grandmothers in black families is unquestioned (Billingsley 1992; Frazier 1939; Hill 1971; Ladner 1971; Ladner and Gourdine, 1984), however, the contemporary roles and challenges present serious consequences, if not a threat, to the strong tradition of African American families.

African American families have traditionally been described as extended family networks with a lot of cooperation and support. However, Burton (1992) found that African American grandmothers were not receiving consistent and reliable support from family members. Minkler and Roe, on the other hand, found that African American grandmothers had a rich social network of family members and friends. To the contrary, however, they also found social isolation among the younger grandmothers who were experiencing role conflict caused by employment and child care (1993). Other psychological responses included feelings of guilt and shame because of the drug use of their children. Raising grandchildren with special needs (Davis 1992; Brown and Monye 1995; Burton 1992; Minkler and Roe 1993), as well as caring for adolescents (Kee 1997), who have their own unique set of needs, all present social, health, and psychological problems for African American grandmothers.

In their exploratory study of physical and emotional health of African American grandmothers, Minkler, Roe, and Price (1992), using a self-rated measure, found that 44 percent of the respondents stated that they were in pain at the time of the interview; 49 percent had back pain; and 25 percent had heart trouble. Slightly over one-third reported worsening of existing poor health. Fifty-four percent of the sample reported being in good or excellent physical health, and almost half stated that their health never interfered with their caregiving roles. A number of other health problems, such as depression, insomnia, hypertension, stomach pain, and other problems associated with the physical and emotional demands of child care have been reported (Minkler and Roe 1996), however, grandmothers tended to minimize the severity of the health problems in an effort to show that they were capable of taking care of their grandchildren. Changes in social behaviors, such as an increase in cigarette smoking and alcohol use, are also associated with the demands of caring for grandchildren (Burton

1992; Minkler and Roe 1996; Minkler, Roe, and Price 1992). It is not easy to overlook the stressors and problems associated with grandmothers caring for their grandchildren; and with the increase in AIDS, crack cocaine use, and the incarceration of the parents of the grandchildren, custodial grandmothers face escalating financial and social burdens. Although the contemporary problems and role responsibilities have changed for African American grandmothers, the commitment they have for their grandchildren is intimately connected to her historical role as caretaker and nurturer.

## SUMMARY AND RESEARCH RECOMMENDATIONS

Demographic and socioeconomic trends have changed the structure of the American family. Since 1977, there has been a rapid increase in the number of families maintained by grandparents. This chapter has addressed the rise in grandparent-headed households and some problems associated with raising grandchildren whose parents are incarcerated or addicted to drugs. A number of reasons may account for the rapid increase in households maintained by grandparents. While functioning in the role of surrogate parents in the case of crack-cocaine addiction and the incarceration of their daughters, African American grandmothers experience much stress and many problems. To date, very little systematic research is available on the incidence and prevalence of African American grandmothers who have primary care responsibility for raising their grandchildren. Research on surrogate parenting among grandmothers is a relatively new phenomenon and open to many diverse approaches. The following questions may be considered for study: (1) What is the impact of primary caregiving on the health and well-being of African American grandmothers? (2) What are the incidence and prevalence rates of grandparents who care for their grandchildren in African American communities? (3) How does the impact of incarcerations, drug addiction, and HIV/AIDS affect surrogate parenting among African American grandmothers? (4) Are there differences in caregiving in rural and urban areas? (5) What is the influence of different levels of caregiving on stress and depression? (6) What are the sources and types of social support received by grandmother caregivers? It is anticipated that findings from research studies presented in this chapter will motivate other social scientists to seriously explore some of the issues involved in surrogate parenting among African American grandmothers.

# 3

# Methodology: The Custodial African American Grandmother Study

## SAMPLE

A cross-sectional design was used to examine demographic characteristics, health, and psychological well-being among African American grandmothers who have primary responsibility for raising their grandchildren. The study population consisted of ninety-nine custodial African American grandmothers who resided in the Triangle and Piedmont areas of North Carolina. Grandmothers who were eligible for the study were required to meet the following criteria: (1) They were the primary caregivers for one or more children under age eighteen; (2) they were noninstitutionalized; (3) they were residents of the Triangle and Piedmont areas of North Carolina, and; (4) they viewed themselves as being in grandparenting relationships with their grandchildren.

## DATA COLLECTION

Five North Carolina counties were involved in the study. These included Durham, Guilford, Mecklenburg, Orange, and Wake. A number of organizations and persons provided assistance in identifying grandmothers who met the study criteria. North Carolina Division on Aging, Durham County Social Services, Durham County Housing Authority, Orange County Housing Authority, senior centers, support groups, churches, community nurses, mental health centers, family social workers in public schools, and juvenile detention facilities were among the agencies involved. Representatives from these agencies were asked to identify grandmothers within their agencies who were custodial caregivers for at least one grandchild. The study also used word-of-mouth recruitment through local African American churches, cultural community organizations, and grandparent participants. After a list of grandmothers had been identified, those who expressed an interest in the study were prescreened to determine their eligibility for inclusion. Once the inclusion criteria were satisfied, appointments were made to meet with the grandparent at a location convenient to the subject. Most of the interviews ($n = 90$) took place in the subjects' homes, with the exception of a few ($n = 9$) who were interviewed at support group meetings or other locations designated by the respondent.

The data collection instrument was pretested using a focus group of ten grandmother caregivers, to eliminate any difficult questions, and to make the protocol more understandable and relevant to this sample. All interviews were conducted by the author between August 1999 and November 2000. Most interviews took from two to three hours each to complete. However, it was not unusual for an interview to take as long as four or five hours depending on the openness and personality of the grandmother. This was the only opportunity for many grandmothers to discuss their experiences and vent their difficulties and frustrations. In approximately 20 percent of the cases, where an interview became too extensive, a follow-up meeting was scheduled or completed over the telephone. These were instances where the grandchild may have returned from school and needed the attention of the grandmother or the grandchild's parent may have entered the home and the grandmother did not wish to discuss her child care burdens in her or his presence. Because of the demanding work schedules of some grandmothers, telephone interviews were necessary.

### Measures

The Institutional Review Board of Duke University Medical Center approved the instrument used in this study. The instrument consisted of approximately 350 questions comprised of primarily quantitative information, and approximately 30 questions consisted of qualitative information. The major issues discussed in the questionnaire included the following eleven components: demographic characteristics, household composition, economic resources, family competing demands, reasons for providing care, church and social support, value orientation and family relationships, physical health and chronic conditions, life satisfaction, depression, and stress symptoms. All but stress symptoms are included in this analysis.

## Demographic and Social Characteristics

The demographic characteristics include age, income, education, marital status, sources of income, religiosity, and household composition. Reasons for providing care is a listing of sixteen reasons and each respondent was asked to check only those that were relevant to her situation. Besides caring for grandchildren and great-grandchildren, grandmothers may also have competing family demands, which might require caring for a sick husband, ailing parents, or some other family member. Grandmothers were asked to respond to questions pertaining to their caregiving responsibilities, their thoughts and feelings regarding caregiving, and their value system regarding the role of caregiving in families. Additionally, relationship questions were asked related to the quality of the relationship between the child and grandmother, the child and the biological father, the child and the biological mother, and the grandmother and the son or daughter of the child/children. Religious participation consisted of a set of questions about church participation and involvement. These included church membership, frequency of church attendance, and frequency of participation in church service and related church activities. They were asked about the extent to which their spiritual beliefs helped in providing care for their grandchildren.

## Physical Health

This measure consisted of a list of physical health conditions that the respondent might have (Brown and Monye 1995). The conditions included arthritis, cancer, stroke, diabetes, problems breathing, high blood pressure, circulation problems, heart problems, glaucoma, and kidney disease.

## Psychological Health

Psychological health was measured by a modification of the Center for Epidemiological Studies Depression Scale (CES-D) (Radloff 1977). There were no changes in the content of the questions. All questions from the CES-D were included in their original version. However, the response categories were combined into a yes/no format for reporting the presence or absence of a symptom during the week preceding the interview. The revised instrument has been tested extensively by Duke University investigators (Blazer, Burchett, Service, and George 1991) to determine its comparability to the original CES-D Scale. Their results indicate that the modified instrument was virtually identical to the original instrument. Previous studies have shown that a score of 16 on the original scale represents clinically significant depressive symptom (Radloff 1977). Blazer et al. (1991) showed that a score of 9 or greater on the revised scale was equivalent to the score of greater than or equal to 16 on the original scale. Accordingly, we use a dichotomous variable with a score of 9 or greater to indicate the presence of depressive symptoms in the sample.

# 4

# Social and Demographic Characteristics

Demographic and social changes have altered the structure of American families. There has been a drastic increase in grandparent-headed households over the last three decades. There has also been a concurrent increase in the number of single-parent households maintained by grandparents without either biological parent present. The traditional roles of grandmothers have changed from helpers to primary caregivers, in cases where parents are either not able or not willing to take care of their own children. The shift in the roles of grandparents is caused by a number of reasons that were discussed earlier. Some of the more devastating reasons—crack cocaine, AIDS, and incarcerations—have placed an enormous burden on custodial African American grandmothers who may not be prepared economically, physically, or emotionally to care for unexpected grandchildren.

Table 4.1 shows social and demographic characteristics of the ninety-nine grandmothers included in this study. The grandmothers ranged in age from 38 to 88 with an average age of 57. In this sample, 65 percent were 45 to 64 years old; 20 percent were considered elderly ranging in age from 65 to 74; and 6 percent were among the oldest-old (75 and older). The average level of education was 11.5: 36 percent were high school graduates, 38 percent were high school drop-outs, and 25 percent received some college education. Almost three quarters of grandmothers were unmarried and heads of household. Just over half of the grandmothers were retired. Many grandparents had full-time and/or part-time employment: 29 percent were employed full time, and 9 percent were employed part time. The

**TABLE 4.1** Sociodemographic Characteristics of African American Caregiving Grandmothers ($n = 99$)

| Variables | Mean (s.d.) |
| --- | --- |
| Age | 57.6 (10.1) |
|    Younger than 45 (%) | 8.1 |
|    45–54 (%) | 35.4 |
|    55–64 (%) | 30.3 |
|    65–74 (%) | 20.2 |
|    75 or older (%) | 6.1 |
| Years of schooling completed | 11.5 (2.6) |
|    Less than high school (%) | 38.4 |
|    High school graduate (%) | 36.4 |
|    Some college (%) | 21.2 |
|    College graduate (%) | 4.0 |
| Marital status (%) | |
|    Married | 26.3 |
|    Divorced/separated | 40.4 |
|    Widowed | 22.2 |
|    Never married | 11.1 |
| Years lived in current home | 14.5 (11.2) |
| Employment status (%) | |
|    Retired | 51.5 |
|    Full-time | 29.3 |
|    Part-time | 9.1 |
|    Not employed | 9.1 |
|    Other | 3.0 |
| Family income (in 1998 dollars) | |
|    Income (in thousands of dollars) | 21.1 (16.0) |
|    Median income (in thousands of dollars) | 17.5 |
|    Less than $5,000 (%) | 11.1 |
|    $5,000–$10,000 (%) | 22.2 |
|    $10,000–$15,000 (%) | 15.2 |
|    $15,000–$20,000 (%) | 9.1 |
|    $20,000–$30,000 (%) | 15.2 |
|    $30,000–$40,000 (%) | 11.1 |
|    Greater than $40,000 (%) | 16.2 |
| Sources of income (%) | |
|    Wages and salaries | 53.5 |
|    Social security (excluding SSI) | 43.4 |
|    Welfare payments/Work First | 38.4 |
|    Retirement pension | 23.2 |
|    Disability payments | 15.2 |
|    SSI | 13.1 |
|    Assistance from family members or other sources | 6.1 |

(Continued)

**TABLE 4.1   Continued**

| Variables | Mean (s.d.) |
| --- | --- |
| Wealth (%) | |
| Own home | 56.6 |
| Own any other real estate | 16.2 |
| Religion (%) | |
| Baptist | 55.6 |
| Methodist | 11.1 |
| Other religion | 25.3 |
| No religion | 8.1 |

remaining 9 percent who reported that they were neither employed nor retired were grandmothers who had never been in the paid workforce.

The average family income in this sample of grandmothers was $21,100, with a median income of $17,500 (1998 dollars). Of these, 11 percent had annual incomes below $5,000; 22 percent had incomes between $5,001 and $10,000; 24 percent between $10,001 and $20,000; 15 percent between $20,001 and $30,000, 11 percent between $30,001 and $40,000; and 16 percent greater than $40,000. The higher incomes were associated with married grandmothers, or grandmother-maintained households consisting of employed adult children. Of the grandmothers in this study, 54 percent received incomes from wages and salaries; 43 percent from social security; 38 percent from Work First (Social Services); 23 percent from retirement pensions; 15 percent from disability payments; 13 percent from Supplemental Social Security Income; and 6 percent from relatives or other sources. Close to 57 percent owned their own homes, and 16 percent reported owning other real estate property. Most of the home owners lived in rural North Carolina, primarily in mobile homes.

Religion was very important to the women in this study. More than half the sample were Baptist (57 percent); 11 percent Methodist; 25 percent reported religious affiliations other than Baptist or Methodist, such as Catholic, Lutheran, Muslim, Pentecostal, Presbyterian, and Holiness. Only a small number of grandmothers in the sample (8 percent) were not church members. However, regardless of their church membership, all grandmothers said that their spiritual beliefs were very important in providing care to their grandchildren. Typical responses were, "prayer keeps me going," "without God, I don't know what I would do," "my belief in God helps me to discipline better," and "my spiritual beliefs give me more patience."

The family structure among grandmother-maintained households was a combination of spouses, grandchildren, great-grandchildren, coresident children, fictive kin, nieces, nephews, parents, and other relatives. Table 4.2 shows the composition of coresident children and grandchildren in families of African American caregiving grandmothers. The average household consisted of three persons; almost 57 percent of the grandmothers were caring for grandchildren without any adult children in the household; 27 percent had one or two adult daughters in the household; 10 percent lived with a son only; and 5 percent lived with both sons and daughters in the household.

Although the coresident adult child may or may not be the biological parent of all grandchildren the grandmother cared for, he or she was, in most cases, the parent for at least one of the grandchildren. The majority of the grandmothers cared for two or more grandchildren; 36 percent cared for one grandchild only; 22 percent were providing care for granddaughters only; 29 percent were providing care for grandsons only; and

TABLE 4.2    Composition of Coresident Children and Grandchildren in Families of African American Caregiving Grandmothers, Excluding Spouses ($n = 99$)

| Variables | Mean (s.d.) |
|---|---|
| Total number of coresident persons | 2.9 (1.6) |
| Composition of coresident children (%) | |
| None | 56.6 |
| Daughters only | |
| One | 22.2 |
| Two | 5.1 |
| Sons only | |
| One | 10.1 |
| Both daughters and sons | |
| One daughter and one son | 3.0 |
| One daughter and three sons | 1.0 |
| Two daughters and one son | 1.0 |
| Composition of coresident grandchildren (%) | |
| Granddaughters only | |
| One | 16.2 |
| Two or more | 6.1 |
| Grandsons only | |
| One | 20.2 |
| Two or more | 9.1 |
| Both granddaughters and grandsons | |
| One granddaughter and one grandson | 16.2 |
| One granddaughter and two or more grandsons | 11.1 |
| Two or more granddaughters and one grandson | 4.0 |
| Two or more granddaughters and grandsons each | 8.1 |

the remaining 40 percent were providing care for both granddaughters and grandsons. Approximately 25 percent of the grandmothers were providing care for more than three grandchildren in their households.

Table 4.3 shows the average age of the grandchild and years of caregiving among African American grandmothers. The majority of grandmothers in the study had taken care of their grandchildren from birth or shortly thereafter. We examined the age distribution of grandchildren and the number of years the grandmother had been providing care. The average grandchild living in the grandmother's household was 9 years old; 19 percent of the children being raised by grandmothers were 4 or younger; 39 percent were between 5 and 10 years old; 37 percent were between 11 and 17; and a much smaller percentage (4.5 percent) were 18 or older. Grandmothers in this sample took care of their grandchildren for an average of seven years. Almost 12 percent of the grandchildren had been taken care of by their grandmother for less than one year and another 12 percent had been taken care of from one to two years. About 18 percent had been taken care of from three to four years. The majority of the grandchildren had been in their grandmothers' care for five years or longer: 26 percent from five to nine years and 34 percent for ten or more years. It is common for African American grandmothers to care for their grandchildren for long periods of time. And, in cases where grandmothers are primary caregivers because of the drug use, abandonment, incarceration, and AIDS of the grandchildren's parents, it is likely that the majority of the placements will be permanent.

Grandmothers often reported multiple reasons for providing care to their grandchildren (Table 4.4). The primary reason was abuse of drugs and alcohol (45 percent) by the parents of the grandchildren. This is also the

TABLE 4.3    Average Age of Grandchild and Years of Caregiving Reported by African American Caregiving Grandmothers (*n* = 99)

| Variables | Mean (s.d.) |
|---|---|
| Age of grandchild | 9.4 (4.9) |
|    Younger than 4 years old (%) | 19.4 |
|    5–10 (%) | 38.8 |
|    11–17 (%) | 36.9 |
|    18 or older (%) | 4.9 |
| Years of caregiving | 6.9 (5.0) |
|    Less than 1 year (%) | 11.7 |
|    1–2 (%) | 11.7 |
|    3–4 (%) | 17.5 |
|    5–9 (%) | 25.7 |
|    10 or more (%) | 33.5 |

TABLE 4.4   Reasons for Providing Care for Grandchildren
Reported by African American Caregiving Grandmothers ($n = 99$)

| Grandchild's parent | Percentage |
| --- | --- |
| Abused alcohol and drugs | 45.5 |
| Neglected child's needs | 38.4 |
| Needed to work | 23.3 |
| Teenager | 18.2 |
| Had emotional/mental problems | 17.2 |
| Incarcerated | 12.1 |
| Deceased | 10.1 |
| Divorced | 4.1 |
| Needed a break | 3.0 |
| Has AIDS | 3.0 |
| Physically disabled | 2.0 |
| Mentally abused child | 2.0 |
| In school | 1.0 |
| Sexually abused child | 1.0 |
| Other reasons | 30.3 |

number one reason reported in the literature (Burton 1992; Minkler and Roe 1993; Minkler, Roe, and Price 1992; Roe, Minkler, and Barnhill 1994). The next most often reported reason for grandchild care was parents neglecting the grandchild's needs, consisting of 38 percent of the sample. Other reasons included the parent's need to work (23 percent); teen pregnancy (18 percent), parent's emotional or mental problems (17 percent), parent deceased (10 percent), and parent's incarceration (12 percent).

A combined 16 percent reported taking care of their grandchildren because of a parent's divorce, a parent needing a break, AIDS, physical disability of parent, mental and sexual abuse of child, and a parent attending school. The parent's need to work (10 percent) was the most often reported reason for providing care among part-time caregivers. Almost one-third (30 percent) of the sample reported taking care of their grandchildren for other reasons than those listed on the questionnaire. Reasons in this category consisted of financial problems, such as the mother of the child not being able to afford a place to live. It should be noted that these reported reasons are mutually exclusive experiences. Parents' abuse of drugs and alcohol, neglecting the grandchild's needs, and incarcerations were particularly highly correlated.

## DISCUSSION

The primary purpose of this chapter was to provide a sociodemographic profile of custodial African grandmothers. There are more grandmother-headed households in African American families and households with neither biological parent present are relatively common (Szinovacz 1998).

We found that almost 57 percent of the grandmothers were caring for grandchildren without any adult children in the household. Approximately 25 percent of the sample were providing care for more than three grandchildren who lived in the home.

Previous studies document custodial grandparenting as a long-term, labor-intensive commitment (Fuller-Thomson, Minkler, and Driver 1997; Pruchno 1999). Fuller-Thomson (1997) found that more than half of the caregiving grandparents in her study provided custodial care for three years or longer; and 20 percent took care of their grandchildren for more than ten years. Pruchno (1999) reported that grandparents provided primary care for an average of seven years. We found that 34 percent of the grandchildren had been in their grandmothers' care for ten or more years; another 26 percent had been cared for from five to nine years. Regardless of the reasons, in this sample of African American grandmothers, it was a common practice for them to care for their grandchildren for long periods of time. And, in cases where grandmothers are primary caregivers because of drug use of the parent, the placements were more likely to be permanent. Many of the grandmothers had assumed care of their grandchildren from birth or shortly thereafter. Four grandmothers had taken care of their grandchildren for from eighteen to twenty years. Many grandmothers who are primary caregivers were not prepared for this life change, and had ambivalent feelings about their obligations. Their new role was a blessing as well as a burden. Anger and resentment was not uncommon among the younger working grandmothers. As one energetic 47-year-old grandmother describes her situation:

I truly love my grandchildren, but I never wanted to become a mother all over again. I have lost my life. This is not the way I planned my life at this point. I am very resentful that I am in this situation. I hate my daughter for not taking responsibility for her children. I do not want to take care of my grandchildren. It has put me in poverty and caused me to be depressed.

Although many grandparents did not want to care for their grandchildren full-time, they stated that they took their grandchildren because they did not want them to be in foster care. Their general concern for their grandchildren was for their safety and care. Many stated that they wanted their grandchildren to be cared for as well as their own children were.

However, assuming the grandparenting role presented a number of problems for caregivers. Problems included not having enough money to get the things they needed, not having enough time for themselves, not being able to attend church, lost friendships, the need for after school and summer programs, poor health, inability to discipline properly, inability to negotiate school problems, lack of cooperation and support from parents, lack of parental involvement in the child's life, and social abuse from the grandparents' children.

Multiple school suspensions were high among grandchildren cared for by grandmothers. This problem is made more complex among some grandparents who are not able to articulate their needs to school teachers and staff. Often the reasons for suspensions do not get addressed until after the suspension period, which could be up to two weeks depending on the alleged offense. In cases where grandparents are elderly, this problem along with many others become much more serious for the grandchild as well as the grandparent caregiver. Twenty-six percent of the grandparents in our study were 65 and older. The vast majority of the children in this study were born to single mothers. Most children did not know their father or had little or no contact with him, and had little or no relationship with their mother. In cases where there was a relationship with the mother, it was often inconsistent and strained. More research is needed to address the complex social interactions between grandchildren and parents, and how they might affect the long-term success of children who are in the care of grandparents.

All but a few grandmothers in this sample stated that they felt overwhelmed by responsibility. Burton (1992) found that grandparents frequently requested respite care for parenting. However, out of guilt that they might have failed as parents, and out of fear that child protection agencies might remove the children from their care, these grandmothers are often reluctant to seek opportunities for a break. In comparison to their younger counterparts, the older African American grandmothers in this study report feeling less overwhelmed by responsibility, and their attitudes about caregiving were generally more approving. Older African American women place caregiving at the forefront of their existence. Caregiving helps older African American women define who they are and their worth in society. The sacrifices they make for their children and grandchildren are central to their belief system concerning their roles as women and their devotion to children, which is shaped by their West African heritage. Older women's beliefs about family, and the extended family network, have a strong influence on their attitudes about caregiving roles. Although the support of the extended family has a long history in Black American culture, it can no longer shield grandmothers from the burdens and stresses of caregiving brought on by the crack-cocaine epidemic, AIDS, and the incarceration of young African American mothers. Once the norm in African American families, changes in family structure and the impact of societal problems have contributed to the erosion of extended family support.

The head of household status of the grandmother increases her role responsibilities within the family unit. She is not only the "guardian of the generations" as described by E. Franklin Frazier (1939); in our study, she describes herself as caretaker, nurturer, role model, setter of family values, maid, spiritual teacher, advisor, leader, source of wisdom, one who keeps the family together, financial provider, social and emotional supporter, mother, father, and everything to everybody. In spite of her age, frailty, or financial status, the custodial African American grandmother is typically depended upon by all members within the family unit, including grown children not living in the home. African American grandmothers not only provide social, emotional, and financial support to their children, they also serve as enablers for them which encourages dependency. One frail 78-year-old grandmother would do the laundry for a grown healthy daughter using wash tubs. Aware that her mother did not have laundry facilities, the daughter did not seem to be concerned about how the job got done. Another elderly grandmother cared for three teenage boys, while her son lived in the home providing no financial support and no child care assistance. Grandparents were routinely taken advantage of by their own children. However, in spite of the overwhelming responsibility, African American grandmothers take pride in their role as caregivers.

## NOTE

Parts of this chapter were previously published as D. S. Ruiz, C. W. Zhu, and M. R. Crowther, "Social, Demographic, and Health Characteristics of Custodial African American Grandmothers," in *Victimizing Vulnerable Groups: Images of Uniquely High Risk Crime Targets*, ed. C. Coston (Westport, CT: Praeger, 2004).

# 5

# Factors Influencing Life Satisfaction among African American Grandmothers Raising Grandchildren

The Life Satisfaction Index–version A (LSIA), originally constructed by Neugarten, Havighurst, and Tobin (1961) was administered to assess general morale and satisfaction with life among the grandmothers in this sample. The LSIA is a twenty-item questionnaire that covers general feelings of well-being among older adults and has been widely used as an index of quality of life (Adams 1969; Hoyt and Creech 1983; Liang 1984) and has demonstrated validity in studies of stress, coping, and illness among older women (Haley et al. 1995; Lohr, Essex, and Klein 1988). Each item was measured on a five-point Likert scale, with response categories of strongly agree, agree, not sure, disagree, and strongly disagree. Twelve positively worded items were coded as "1" for responses of strongly agree or agree and "0" otherwise; eight negatively worded items were coded as "1" for responses of strongly disagree or disagree and "0" otherwise. A higher score is assumed to mean a higher degree of life satisfaction.

### Demographic and Social Characteristics

Age, education, marital status, employment status, family income, home ownership, religiosity, social support, and the grandmother's caregiving situation were included in the analysis. Religiosity was measured by the number of times per month grandmothers usually went to a place of worship and whether they received any help from their place of worship in caring for their grandchildren. Social support was measured by the number of people on whom grandmothers reported they could rely for help. The grandmother's caregiving situation was measured by the number and age of grandchildren she was caring for and years of care provision.

## Physical Health

This measure consisted of the number of chronic conditions the grandmother might have (Brown and Monye 1995). The chronic conditions included arthritis, cancer, stroke, diabetes, breathing problems, high blood pressure, circulation problems, heart problems, glaucoma, and kidney disease.

## Analysis

We examined life satisfaction of grandmothers by sociodemographic and physical health characteristics and tested differences between groups using analysis of variance (ANOVA). Variables that were significantly correlated with the grandmothers' life satisfaction were then entered in an ordinary least squares regression equation to examine the independent effects of each variable. STATA program was used for computations (StataCorp, 1994).

## RESULTS

The mean score of LSIA in this sample was 12.0 (standard deviation = 3.5). Bivariate analysis (Table 5.1) indicated life satisfaction was positively associated with grandmother's age ($p = 0.05$), education level ($p = 0.01$), and family income ($p = 0.02$). Life satisfaction was negatively associated with grandmother's physical health ($p = 0.01$) and number of grandchildren ($p = 0.05$). There was a trend to significance between life satisfaction and home ownership ($p = 0.09$), and years of care provision ($p = 0.09$). Grandmothers' marital status, employment status, social network, frequency of attending church, and age of grandchildren were not associated with their reports of life satisfaction scores.

Consistent with other studies, Chronbach's alpha was 0.81, suggesting satisfactory internal consistency of the scale (Wallace and Wheeler 2002). As expected, life satisfaction and depression, as measured by CES-D (Radloff 1977), were negatively correlated ($r = -0.48$, $p = 0.001$). The magnitude of correlation, however, suggests that they may assess somewhat different aspects of psychological well-being.

Table 5.2 shows grandmothers' sources of satisfaction. Almost all of the grandmothers (98 percent) believed that compared to other people their age they made a good appearance (Question 15). The great majority (95 percent) also reported that they expected some interesting and pleasant

TABLE 5.1   Sociodemographic Characteristics of African American Caregiving
Grandmothers (*n* = 99)

| Variables | Life satisfaction index—A | |
|---|---|---|
| | Mean | s.d. |
| Sample | 12.0 | 3.5 |
| Age* | | |
| Younger than 65 | 11.6 | 3.6 |
| 65 or older | 13.0 | 2.9 |
| Years of schooling completed* | | |
| Less than high school | 11.4 | 3.5 |
| High school graduate or higher | 13.5 | 2.8 |
| Marital status | | |
| Married | 12.2 | 2.9 |
| Divorced/separated | 11.5 | 3.6 |
| Widowed | 12.6 | 3.8 |
| Never married | 11.7 | 3.7 |
| Employment status | | |
| Retired | 11.7 | 3.7 |
| Full-time | 12.4 | 3.3 |
| Part-time | 11.3 | 3.0 |
| Not employed | 13.6 | 3.2 |
| Other | 10.0 | 4.4 |
| Family income* | | |
| Less than $10,000 | 10.6 | 3.9 |
| $10,001–$20,000 | 11.6 | 3.0 |
| $20,001–$30,000 | 12.6 | 3.7 |
| $30,001–$40,000 | 12.8 | 3.0 |
| Greater than $40,000 | 14.0 | 2.2 |
| Home ownership | | |
| Own home | 12.4 | 3.1 |
| Rent | 11.3 | 3.8 |
| Go to church weekly or more often** | | |
| Yes | 12.3 | 3.1 |
| No | 10.6 | 4.3 |
| Number of people can count on for help* | | |
| None | 11.6 | 3.4 |
| 1–2 | 11.4 | 3.4 |
| 3 or more | 13.1 | 3.5 |
| Number of grandchildren* | | |
| One | 12.6 | 3.2 |
| Two or more | 11.3 | 3.7 |
| Age of grandchild | | |
| 5 or younger | 11.0 | 2.6 |
| 6–11 | 12.0 | 3.9 |
| 12–17 | 12.3 | 3.3 |
| 18 or older | 12.5 | 3.7 |

(Continued)

TABLE 5.1    Continued

| Variables | Life satisfaction index—A | |
|---|---|---|
| | Mean | s.d. |
| Years of caring for grandchild* | | |
|   2 or fewer | 10.7 | 3.0 |
|   3–9 | 12.1 | 3.5 |
|   10 or more | 12.6 | 3.5 |
| Number of chronic conditions* | | |
|   0 | 11.9 | 2.8 |
|   1–2 | 10.9 | 3.0 |
|   3 or more | 10.2 | 4.2 |

TABLE 5.2    Sources of Satisfaction of African American Caregiving
Grandmothers (n = 99)

| Question Number | Source | % |
|---|---|---|
| 1 | As I grow older things seem better than I thought they would be. | 66.7 |
| 2 | I have gotten more of the breaks in life than most of the people I know. | 64.6 |
| 3 | This is the dreariest time of my life. | 19.2 |
| 4 | I am just as happy as when I was younger. | 55.6 |
| 5 | My life could be happier than it is now. | 28.3 |
| 6 | These are the best years of my life. | 58.6 |
| 7 | Most of the things I do are boring or monotonous. | 79.8 |
| 8 | I expect some interesting and pleasant things to happen to me in the future. | 94.9 |
| 9 | The things I do are as interesting to me as they ever were. | 70.7 |
| 10 | I feel old and somewhat tired. | 56.6 |
| 11 | I feel my age but it does not bother me. | 55.6 |
| 12 | As I look back on my life I am fairly well satisfied. | 80.8 |
| 13 | I would not change my past life even if I could. | 56.6 |
| 14 | Compared to other people my age I've made a lot of foolish decisions in my life. | 52.5 |
| 15 | Compared to other people my age I make a good appearance. | 98.0 |
| 16 | I have made plans for things I'll be doing a month or a year from now. | 49.5 |
| 17 | When I think back over my life I didn't get most of the important things I wanted. | 44.4 |
| 18 | Compared to other people I get down in the dumps too often. | 78.8 |
| 19 | I've gotten pretty much what I expected out of life. | 55.6 |
| 20 | In spite of what people say the lot of the average man is getting worse, not better. | 29.3 |

things to happen them her in the future (Question 8). More than 80 percent also reported that looking back on their lives they were fairly satisfied (Question 12). The most common sources of dissatisfaction include that most of the things the grandmothers did were boring or monotonous (80 percent, Question 7) and that compared to other people they got down in the dumps too often (80 percent, Question 18).

An ordinary least squares (OLS) regression model was conducted to examine the independent effects of each variable on the grandmothers' life satisfaction (Table 5.3). Consistent with results from the bivariate analyses, older age ($p = 0.006$), higher education ($p = 0.04$), higher income ($p = 0.008$), fewer chronic conditions ($p = 0.008$), and years of care provision ($p = 0.006$) were associated with higher life satisfaction. Home ownership, number of grandchildren under the grandmothers' care, frequency of attending church, were no longer statistically significant and were dropped from the model.

The mean score of LSIA in this sample of caregiving grandmothers was 12.0, similar to those obtained from other populations using the twenty-item scale and two-point responses (Adams 1969; Neugarten, Havinghurst, and Tobin 1991). The grandmothers in this sample were mobile, generally healthy, and had few debilitating problems.

Consistent with other studies, a number of sociodemographic characteristics are associated with life satisfaction. Similar to existing literature (Neighbors 1986; Tran, Wright, and Chatters 1991; Utsey, Payne, Jackson, and Jones 2002), results of this study show that low levels of income and education and poor physical health were associated with lower levels of life satisfaction.

In addition to these variables known to influence grandparents' life satisfaction, results in this study also found that years of providing care to grandchildren was positively associated with grandmothers' life satisfaction. This result is consistent with the notion that despite the multiple stresses that caregiving grandparents face, grandparenting has many rewards, yields greater life satisfaction, and provides a positive influence

TABLE 5.3  Predictors of Life Satisfaction (LSIA) among African American Caregiving Grandmothers ($n = 99$)

| Variables | Coefficient | Standard error |
|---|---|---|
| Age 65 or older = 1 | 2.06*** | 0.734 |
| Less than high school education = 1 | −1.51** | 0.745 |
| Income less than $20,000 = 1 | −1.83*** | 0.670 |
| Number of chronic conditions | −0.53*** | 0.195 |
| Years of providing care to grandchild | 0.19*** | 0.067 |
| Constant | 13.35 | 0.783 |

Note.** significant at 5% level, *** significant at 1% level.

on the other generations within the family (Davidhizar, Bechtel, and Woodring 2000; Emick and Hayslip 1996; Forsyth, Roberts, and Robin 1992). Grandparenting may be serving a compensatory function with respect to life satisfaction.

Sarah, a 63-year-old grandmother, has been taking care of her grand-daughter for six years, because of drug use of her parents. Initially, Sarah had mixed feelings about taking full responsibility for the care of her granddaughter, but "after taking time to prepare psychologically for the challenge," she concluded that it was in the best interest of the child. Sarah discusses the circumstances that led to her assuming care of her granddaughter,

My granddaughter's parents were not married when she was conceived. Her father deserted her mother, and the mother was about to put her up for adoption. She was being shifted from place to place. I wanted to provide a stable life for her. She needed a family to care for her. I was not planning to do this at this time in my life. I have adjusted to her, and I feel good about it now. I enjoy sharing with her and doing things with her. There is power in raising children, because Black women have never had power outside the home. The power in the home is the only power she has known.

Daisy, a 48-year-old grandmother, has been primary caregiver for her granddaughter since birth, and has taken care of her 10-year-old grandson for seven years. When asked what lead to her decision to take care of her grandchildren, she responds:

They were living in poor conditions. My 26-year-old daughter could not take care of the children well. There was a lot of stress and pressure on her, and she had problems taking care of my sick granddaughter who is retarded. Their mother is not financially able to take care of the children, and I did not want them to be neglected.

Her concern for her grandchildren is similar to many grandmothers in the study who feel that they can do a better job of raising their grandchildren than their daughters. They also feel strongly about giving their grandchildren the opportunities, safe environments, and supports they gave their own children.

Laura, a 46-year-old grandmother, who has taken care of her grandchildren for all of their lives, assumed care because of their mother's alcohol and drug use. She takes pride in caring for her grandchildren. She says,

They are my children and I love to see them grow. But, this is not the way I'd hoped. The values we taught our children did not turn out the way we thought. I feel like I've been a parent for a long time. Everything happens for a reason.

In spite of the intensity of their feelings, however, grandmothers in the study generally assumed care, and remained in the role of caregiving for a number of reasons. These included (1) a deeply felt sense of obligation to their grandchildren, (2) the need to keep their grandchildren out of the system, (3) the need to control the "proper" upbringing of the child, and (4) the need to care for others. Although placing the grandchild with the grandmother might seem to be the most likely alternative, some grandparents are old, frail, and are not prepared to care for children with severe emotional, social, and/or physical disabilities that are characteristic of many of the grandchildren in this study. However, in spite of health, economic, or social problems, the majority of the grandmothers enjoyed taking care of their grandchildren, and felt blessed to have them.

# 6

# Social Factors, Health Status, and Depression

This chapter discusses the relationships between social factors, health status, and depression among custodial African American grandmothers. Existing literature has identified some factors that affect depression among grandparents. In their analysis of the second wave of the National Survey of Families and Households, Minkler, Fuller-Thomson, Miller, and Driver (1997), found that depressive symptoms were associated with caring for a grandchild. Other factors found to be associated with low levels of depression included older age, higher family income, greater number and better quality of social networks, being married, and being in excellent health. Although Minkler and associates (1997) found an inverse relationship between age and depression, suggesting that grandmothers over 65 seem to be more comfortable with the grandparenting role than younger grandmothers, results from other studies found the relationship between age and depression is not clear (Blazer, Burchett, Service, and George 1991; Raymond and Michaels 1980).

Among African American grandmothers, age may have different effects on depression. In African American communities, older women caring for grandchildren and other relatives is not uncommon (Billingsley 1992). Many have taken care of young relatives for all of their adult life. However, younger grandmothers may not be comfortable with the grandmother roles because of competing factors including employment, competing family demands, active social life, or the need to be involved with their own minor children. There has been little research that examines the associations between custodial caregiving and the onset of depression among African American grandmothers.

Studies have shown that the demands of custodial caregiving among grandparents may affect physical health as well (Burnette 1999; Minkler and Fuller-Thomson 1999; Minkler and Roe 1993; Minkler, Roe, and Price 1992; Musil 1998). In their exploratory study of physical and emotional health of seventy-one African American grandmothers raising their grandchildren because of crack cocaine use of the parents, Minkler, Roe, and Price (1992) found that 44 percent of the respondents were in pain; 49 percent had back pain; and 25 percent had heart trouble. Slightly over one-third of the grandmothers reported that their health worsened after assuming care of their grandchildren. Musil (1998), on the other hand, in a small study of ninety grandmothers, including both whites and blacks, found no differences in physical and emotional health between grandmothers who were primary caregivers and those who were not. To date, results on the relationship between custodial grandparenting and grandmothers' physical health are inconclusive. Even less is known about this relationship among African American grandmothers.

The relationship between social support and depression in later life is well established in the literature (Aneshensel, Frerichs, and Huba 1984; George 1992; Szinovacz, DeViney, and Atkinson 1999). However, the relationship between social support and depression among caregiving grandmothers is less clear. Only a few studies have addressed how the quality and number of supports for grandparent caregivers affect their psychological health (Burnette 1999; Minkler and Roe 1993; Musil 1998; Poe 1992); most of these are the results of qualitative approaches. The general consensus is that support for grandparents is limited (Burnette 1999; Minkler and Roe 1993; Musil 1998). Musil (1998) found that custodial grandmothers reported receiving less instrumental and subjective support than noncustodial grandmothers did. Research on the importance of social support on the current generation of African American grandmothers is sketchy at best.

This chapter will provide insight into relationships between selected social and health variables, and depression among custodial African American grandmothers. The following questions will be addressed: What are some social, demographic, and physical health characteristics of custodial grandmothers? Is depression associated with age of grandmother, age of grandchildren, physical health, and social support?

## Depression

Depressive symptomatology was measured by a modified version of the Center for Epidemiological Studies Depression Scale (CES-D) (Radloff 1977). There were no changes in the content of the questions. All questions from the CES-D were included in their original version. However, instead of the original scale that measured each question in a 0–3 scale, the modified response categories were combined into a yes/no format for reporting the presence or absence of a symptom during the week preceding the interview. The revised instrument has been tested extensively by Duke University investigators (Blazer et al. 1991) to determine its comparability to the original CES-D Scale. Their results indicate that the modified instrument was virtually identical to the original instrument.

Previous studies have shown that a score of 16 or higher on the original scale represents clinically significant depressive symptoms (Radloff 1977). Blazer and associates (1991) showed that a score of 9 or greater on the revised scale was equivalent to the score of greater than or equal to 16 on the original scale. Accordingly, we constructed a dichotomous variable that equals to 1 to indicate depression if the total CES-D score equaled to 9 or greater and 0 if the score was less than 9 to indicate the absence of depressive symptoms.

### Analysis

We examined sociodemographic and physical health characteristics of grandmothers who had depressive symptomatology (reported total CES-D score greater than or equal to 9) and grandmothers who were not depressed (reported total CES-D score less than 9) separately. Student t-tests were used to test for differences in means in the continuous variables and chi-squared tests were used for discrete variables. A logistic regression was performed to examine the effects of sociodemographic and physical health characteristics on depressive symptomatology of the grandmothers. STATA program was used for computations (STATA 1994).

### RESULTS

Table 6.1 shows social and demographic characteristics for grandmothers who had depressive symptoms (CES-D score greater than or equal to 9) and compared them with those who did not (CES-D score less than 9). The majority of the custodial grandmothers in this sample (80 percent) were not depressed, with an average CES-D score of 2.4 (s.d. = 2.4).

Those who were depressed reported an average CES-D score of 13.3 (s.d. = 2.9). Lower CES-D scores were significantly associated with older ages ($p = 0.03$), not receiving social security benefits ($p = 0.007$), receiving disability payments ($p = 0.03$), having a greater number of social supports ($p = 0.01$), having more custodial grandchildren ($p = 0.02$), and caring for older grandchildren ($p = 0.02$). There is a trend toward significance between depression and being divorced or separated ($p = 0.08$), high income ($p = 0.09$), and fewer years of custodial care provision ($p = 0.09$). No associations were found in the bivariate analysis for high school

**TABLE 6.1** Sociodemographic Characteristics of African American Caregiving Grandmothers ($n = 99$)

| Variables | Depression Status | | |
| --- | --- | --- | --- |
| | Sample | Not depressed | Depressed |
| | Mean (s.d.) | Mean (s.d.) | Mean (s.d.) |
| N | 99 | 80 | 19 |
| Mean CES-D score | 4.5 (5.0) | 2.4 (2.4) | 13.3 (2.9) |
| Age (mean years)* | 57.6 (10.1) | 58.6 (10.3) | 53.3 (7.5) |
| Younger than 45 (%) | 8.1 | 7.5 | 10.5 |
| 45–54 (%) | 35.4 | 32.5 | 47.4 |
| 55–64 (%) | 30.3 | 28.8 | 36.8 |
| 65–74 (%) | 20.2 | 23.8 | 5.3 |
| 75 or older (%) | 6.1 | 7.5 | 0.0 |
| Years of schooling completed | 11.5 (2.6) | 11.6 (2.2) | 11.2 (3.8) |
| Less than high school (%) | 38.4 | 37.5 | 42.1 |
| High school graduate (%) | 36.4 | 37.5 | 31.6 |
| Some college (%) | 21.2 | 21.3 | 21.1 |
| College graduate (%) | 4.0 | 3.8 | 5.3 |
| Marital status (%) | | | |
| Married | 26.3 | 28.8 | 15.8 |
| Divorced/separated | 40.4 | 36.3 | 57.9 |
| Widowed | 22.2 | 25.0 | 10.5 |
| Never married | 11.1 | 10.0 | 15.8 |
| Employment status (%) | | | |
| Retired | 51.5 | 50.0 | 57.9 |
| Full-time | 29.3 | 30.0 | 26.3 |
| Part-time | 9.1 | 7.5 | 15.8 |
| Not employed | 9.1 | 11.3 | 0 |
| Other | 3.0 | 2.5 | 5.3 |
| Family income in 1998 (in thousands of dollars) | 21.1 (16.0) | 21.6 (1.7) | 19.1 (4.2) |
| Median (in thousands of dollars) | 17.5 | 17.5 | 12.5 |
| Less than $5,000 | 11.1 | 8.8 | 21.1 |
| $5,001–$10,000 | 22.2 | 21.3 | 26.3 |
| $10,001–$15,000 | 15.2 | 16.3 | 10.5 |
| $15,001–$20,000 | 9.1 | 10.0 | 5.3 |
| $20,001–$30,000 | 15.2 | 15.0 | 15.8 |
| $30,001–$40,000 | 11.1 | 13.8 | 0.0 |
| Greater than $40,000 | 16.2 | 15.0 | 21.1 |
| Sources of income (%) | | | |
| Wages and salaried | 53.5 | 55.0 | 47.4 |
| Social security (Excluding SSI)* | 43.4 | 50.0 | 15.8 |

(Continued)

**TABLE 6.1   Continued**

| Variable | Depression Status | | |
|---|---|---|---|
| | Sample | Not depressed | Depressed |
| Sources of income (%) (continued) | | | |
| Disability payments* | 15.2 | 11.3 | 31.6 |
| Retirement pension | 23.2 | 23.8 | 21.1 |
| Supplemental Security Income | 13.1 | 15.0 | 5.3 |
| Welfare payments/Work first | 38.4 | 35.0 | 52.6 |
| Wealth (%) | | | |
| Own home | 56.6 | 60.0 | 42.1 |
| Own any other real estate | 16.2 | 17.5 | 10.5 |
| Religion (%) | | | |
| Baptist | 55.6 | 57.5 | 47.4 |
| Methodist | 11.1 | 12.5 | 5.3 |
| No religion | 8.1 | 7.5 | 10.5 |
| Other religion | 25.3 | 22.5 | 36.8 |
| Number of people can rely on | 1.8 (1.3) | 1.9 (1.3) | 1.1 (0.9) |
| Number of grandchildren* | 2.0 (1.4) | 1.8 (1.3) | 2.5 (1.7) |
| One (%) | 47.5 | 50.0 | 63.2 |
| Two or more (%) | 52.5 | 50.0 | 36.8 |
| Age of grandchild* | 7.9 (5.2) | 8.5 (5.2) | 5.4 (4.5) |
| 5 or younger | 17.2 | 15.0 | 26.3 |
| 6–11 | 45.5 | 43.8 | 52.6 |
| 12–17 | 29.3 | 31.3 | 21.1 |
| 18 or older | 8.1 | 10.0 | 0 |
| Years of caring for grandchild | 7.3 (4.8) | 7.7 (4.8) | 5.7 (4.7) |
| Two or fewer | 24.2 | 21.3 | 36.8 |
| 3–9 | 42.4 | 42.5 | 42.1 |
| 10 or more | 33.3 | 36.3 | 21.1 |
| Has coresident adult child (%) | 33.3 | 36.3 | 21.1 |
| Age of coresident adult child | 32.2 (7.8) | 31.9 (8.1) | 33.2 (7.2) |

*Notes:*

Standard deviations are shown in parentheses.

Child refers to the grandmothers' adult child.

* Difference between depressed and nondepressed grandmothers statistically significant at 0.05 level.

completion, employment status, home ownership, religious participation, years of caregiving, and having at least one coresident adult child.

Table 6.2 presents bivariate results of physical health status of the custodial grandmother by their depressive symptomatology. Grandmothers who were depressed (having CES-D score 9 or greater) on average had three chronic conditions, one more than grandmothers who were not depressed (p = 0.03). Two-thirds of all grandmothers had high blood pressure and about half had arthritis. Grandmothers who were depressed were more

TABLE 6.2   Physical Health Status of African American Caregiving
Grandmothers (*n* = 99)

| Variables | Depression Status | | |
|---|---|---|---|
| | All sample | Not depressed | Depressed |
| | Mean (s.d.) | Mean (s.d.) | Mean (s.d.) |
| N | 99 | 80 | 19 |
| Number of chronic conditions* | 2.2 (1.6) | 2.1 (1.5) | 3.0 (1.8) |
| High blood pressure | 61.6 | 61.3 | 63.2 |
| Arthritis | 44.4 | 42.5 | 52.6 |
| Problem with breathing* | 25.3 | 20.0 | 47.4 |
| Diabetes | 25.3 | 23.8 | 31.6 |
| Circulation problems | 22.2 | 20.0 | 31.6 |
| Heart problems | 17.2 | 13.8 | 31.6 |
| Glaucoma* | 17.2 | 12.5 | 36.8 |
| Cancer* | 8.1 | 5.0 | 21.1 |
| Stroke | 8.1 | 6.3 | 15.8 |
| Kidney disease* | 7.1 | 3.8 | 21.1 |

*Notes:*

Standard deviations are shown in parentheses.

* Difference between depressed and nondepressed grandmothers statistically significant at
  0.05 level.

likely to report having all ten conditions asked about in the survey. The
differences in the probability of reporting each of the following diseases
was tremendous: Grandmothers who were depressed were more than twice
as likely to report problems with breathing (47 percent vs. 20 percent,
p = 0.01), almost three times as likely to report glaucoma (37 percent vs.
13 percent, p = 0.01), more than twice as likely to report heart problems
(32 percent vs. 14 percent, p = 0.07), more than four times as likely to
report cancer (21 percent vs. 5 percent, p = 0.02), and more than five
times as likely to report kidney disease (21 percent vs. 4 percent,
p = 0.008). Possibly because of the small sample, rates of high blood
pressure, arthritis, circulation problems, diabetes, and stroke were not
significantly different between these two groups.

A logistic regression was performed to determine the relationship
between grandparent caregiving and depression, controlling for sociodemographic factors that have been found to be associated with depressive
symptoms (Table 6.3). The outcome variable is 1 if the grandmother was
depressed (CES-D score greater or equal to 9), and 0 if not depressed
(CES-D score less than 9). The model is highly significant (p < 0.001).
Consistent with results from the bivariate analyses, older age (p < 0.05),
more social support (p < 0.05), and caring for older children (p < 0.05)
are all associated with low levels of depression. Indeed, having one more

TABLE 6.3  Predictors of Depression (CES-D Score Greater Than or Equal to 9) among African American Caregiving Grandmothers ($n = 99$)

| Variables | Coefficient | Standard error | Odds ratio |
|---|---|---|---|
| Age 65 or older = 1 | −2.028** | 1.177 | 0.13 |
| Less than high school education = 1 | −0.388 | 0.683 | 0.68 |
| Married or widowed = 1 | −0.666 | 0.657 | 0.51 |
| Number of chronic conditions | 0.521*** | 0.193 | 1.68 |
| Number of people can rely on | −0.527** | 0.279 | 0.59 |
| Age of youngest grandchild | −0.138** | 0.071 | 0.87 |
| Constant | −0.128 | 0.905 | |
| Prob > $\chi^2$ | 0.0004 | | |

Note: * significant at 10% level; ** significant at 5% level; *** significant at 1% level.

person the grandmother can rely on for help decreased the probability of her being depressed by 41 percent. Not surprisingly, depression was associated with an increased number of chronic conditions ($p < 0.0001$): Having one more chronic condition increased the probability of being depressed by 68 percent. Unfortunately, the size of the sample precluded an analysis of the effects of individual conditions separately. Neither high school completion nor marital status was associated with depression in the logistic regression analysis.

## DISCUSSION

The purpose of this chapter was to make a contribution to the existing research on the impact of social and health factors on custodial African American grandmothers. In spite of the nonrandom, self-selected sample, we believe the results contribute to a better understanding of the experiences of African American grandmothers who are primary caregivers. A bivariate analysis comparing depression scores for selected demographic variables showed low depression scores among grandmothers who were older, married, and had high incomes. Low depression scores were also associated with grandmothers who received social security benefits, had more social support and who cared for older children. In a logistic regression, age, social support, and caring for older children continued to be associated with low levels of depression. High depression scores were associated with increased numbers of chronic health conditions.

Differences in depressive symptomatology by grandmothers' marital status is of note. The majority of the grandmothers in this sample were widowed, divorced, or separated. In our bivariate analysis, a larger proportion of widows were depressed but a smaller proportion of divorced or separated grandmothers were. However, data revealed only a trend toward significance between depression and being divorced or separated, and the difference was no longer significant after controlling for other factors. It appears that in this group of custodial grandmothers, not being married does not have any ill effects in terms of their psychological well-being. The findings from this study are consistent with previous studies showing high rates of depression among women (Beckman and Leber 1995; George 1995; Minkler, Fuller-Thomson, Miller, and Driver 1997). The lower depression scores among older grandmothers is consistent with findings from Minkler et al. (1997). Conflicting role responsibilities are often associated with young grandmothers who may be employed or have minor children of their own.

This chapter has provided a clearer picture of the social, psychological, and physical characteristics of African American grandmothers who are custodial caregivers. Program and policy agenda must address the need to support families headed by single African American grandmothers who have special problems and unusual circumstances. They are at a time in life when they might have expected to be "on their own again," without the child-rearing responsibilities associated with earlier life stages. Grandmothers who do not have a spouse due to death, divorce, or separation would especially expect to be relatively free from family responsibilities. In spite of these expectations, we see that many African American grandmothers take on the demands of caring for young children, often in the face of ill health and reduced social support.

## NOTE

Parts of this chapter were previously published as D. S. Ruiz, C. W. Zhu, and M. R. Crowther, "*Not* on Their Own Again: Psychological, Social, and Health Characteristics of Custodial American Grandmothers," in *Widows and Divorce in Later Life: On Their Own Again,* ed. C. Jenkins (New York: Haworth, 2003).

# 7

# Voices of Custodial Grandmothers: Dominant Themes

The qualitative data analysis consists of fifty of the ninety-nine women in the study. Fifty were selected for analysis because they represented the general problems and issues of the entire sample. Cases were also selected based on their distinctiveness or unusual circumstances of caregiving. Each case includes the following categories of information: household composition, background, circumstances pertaining to the assumption of the caregive role, problems, attitudes and experiences of caregiving, reasons for caregiving, family values, and self-perceptions.

### Alice—Age 69

**Household Composition**

| | |
|---|---|
| Son | 29 |
| Grandson | 14 |
| Grandson | 12 |
| Grandson | 11 |

Alice is a 69-year-old widowed grandmother with a tenth-grade education. She has worked for most of her adult life in child care, as a machine operator, and as a domestic. She is living in a small house that she has lived in for one year. She is retired with an annual income of approximately $16,000 from Social Security, retirement benefits, and Work First. She has four children and eighteen grandchildren. She had her first child when she was 18.

Alice has taken care of all three grandsons since their birth, because of the incarceration of their mother. Although Alice says that she feels good about caring for her grandchildren, a number of problems interfere with her child-care duties. Her major problems, she says, are transportation and lack of financial support. She has discipline problems with her three grandsons. "They need to be in after school activities, like a Big Brother program; they are beginning to talk back and walk out of the house," she says. She also has problems with the school system. The day I visited with her in October, her 11-year-old grandson had been suspended from school for the second time since the beginning of the school year. She was waiting out the two-week suspension period before going in to see the principal. School suspensions among grandchildren in this sample were noticeably high.

Her own 28-year-old son, who lives in the home, aggravates the situation even more, because of his lack of support and involvement in the care of his nephews. She receives no financial support from him, and she is not strong enough to ask him to leave. This is an example where the mother is being an enabler. She is enabling her son to be dependent and irresponsible, as well as allowing him to take advantage of her. This pattern was common among grandmother-headed families where grown children were living in the home.

In spite of the setbacks, however, Alice enjoys raising her grandchildren. She says, "I want to raise my grandchildren. They are my company. I would feel real bad if they were not here. I enjoy family time, conversations with them, and taking them out." Alice does not have anyone to help with her adolescent and teen grandsons. She relies heavily on God through prayer and church involvement. She says that she has excellent relationships with her grandsons, but that they have very poor relationships with their parents.

Alice was raised by her brother and mother. She was taught to believe in God, honesty, respect for parents, and the importance of education. As an adult, she has come to value life and health. She wants her grandsons to get along with each other, stay out of trouble, and believe in God. Alice takes pride in "being there for everybody." She describes herself as a "role model for the entire family."

## Francis—Age 64

### Household Composition

| | |
|---|---|
| Husband | 58 |
| Daughter | 22 |
| Son-in-law | 25 |
| Daughter | 17 |
| Grandson | 1 |

Francis, a 64-year-old married grandmother, is primary caregiver for her 1-year-old grandson. She is a tenth-grade dropout who has worked as a housekeeper for most of her adult life. She has lived for thirty years in a mobile home in Orange County, North Carolina. She is employed part-time in housekeeping, and reports more than $40,000 for their annual household income from earnings and Social Security. She has two children and one grandchild.

Francis cares for her grandchild because his parents need to work. The grandchild's parents reside in the home because they are having financial problems. The grandmother gets little help from the parents in caring for the child. The day that I visited, Francis had just arrived from work. Although the parents as well as the 17-year-old daughter were in the home, she immediately began to feed and care for the child while the child's mother moved carelessly around the house. In spite of the baby's cries and her attempt to assist me with the study, she never asked for assistance from either parent or her teenage daughter. She took care of the baby throughout the two-hour interview. Many household chores needed to be done, yet the young daughter was causally reclining on the sofa watching television. Out of concern, I asked if the teenage daughter was sick. "No" the grandmother answers, "she does this all the time." This is a classic example of the grandmother who performs the role of maid to her children, depriving them of their ability to be creative, independent, and responsible adults.

Although she does not receive much social support within the home, she says that she is very satisfied with the emotional and social support she receives from other family members and friends. She also relies heavily on "prayer and God." She says that her religious beliefs give her "strength and patience."

Francis was raised by her parents in Orange County, North Carolina, who taught her the importance of education and religion. She also values achievement and family. She wants her grandson to know "right from wrong" and learn "good moral behavior." She describes her role as "advisor" and adds, "they look up to me, they can't do without me. I keep my family together."

## Connie—Age 64

### Household Composition

| | |
|---|---|
| Step-granddaughter | 11 |
| Step-granddaughter | 5 |

Connie, a 64-year-old divorced grandmother, cares for her two step-granddaughters in rural North Carolina. She dropped out of high school in the eleventh grade, and has never worked outside of the home. She owns her own home that she has lived in for eighteen years. Her income, less than $7,000 annually, comes from Social Security Supplement and Work First. She has five children and seven grandchildren.

Although she has been blind since age 2, Connie takes care of her two step-granddaughters with help from her companion. She assumed care because of the incarceration of their father, and the physical disability of the mother. Initially, when she took responsibility for the children, their mother was a teen parent. Connie says that she enjoys "doing things for them, but I need more money." She says that the $236 per month that she receives from Work First is not enough to support them. She is also concerned about her health. She says, "as long as God gives me breath, I'll see that they continue to go to school and church." In spite of her disability, however, Connie says that she feels "good" about caring for her step-grandchildren.

Connie receives reliable support from her companion, who helps her with the grandchildren. However, she receives little support from her own children. Her social network is strong, consisting primarily of friends and family. She is a church member and attends services weekly. She feels her spiritual beliefs give her strength. She says, "faith helps me with my grandchildren. I know there is a God." The children receive little or no support from their parents. The father is in jail and the mother has no relationship with the children. She does not call at all. "The saving grace for the grandchildren is the love and support they receive from their step-grandmother."

Connie was raised by her grandparents who taught her never to "lean on people, take care of yourself." Connie values health, children, church, and home. She wants her grandchildren to honor those who are older, get a good education, believe in God, learn to take care of clothes, learn to do for themselves, and help others who don't have as much. She describes herself as, "someone who watches over my grandchildren."

### Martha—Age 61

**Household Composition**

| | |
|---|---|
| Brother | 41 |
| Sister | 38 |
| Fictive kin | 31 |
| Grandson | 18 |
| Grandson | 13 |
| Grandson | 8 |
| Granddaughter | 6 |

This family, headed by a 61-year-old grandmother, consists of the grandmother's siblings, fictive kin, and grandchildren. Martha, who is wheelchair-bound, has never been married and has seven children and thirteen grandchildren. She has worked for most of her life as a cook and housekeeper. She lives in a low-income apartment complex in a small North Carolina town. She reports an annual income of more than $30,000, which comes from her daughter's employment and a retirement pension.

Although Martha weighs over 300 pounds, is wheelchair-bound, and in poor health, she is head of household for four adults and four grandchildren. As custodial caregiver, her duties include doing the laundry, ironing, cooking, cleaning, and providing most of the financial support for the household. Martha has good instrumental support but her emotional support network is weak. Like most of the grandmothers in the study, she relies on herself when something is bothering her, or when she is feeling depressed. She is comforted by her spiritual beliefs. She is a church member, but does not attend services or programs. She watches religious services on television and listens to them on the radio. She says, "my spiritual beliefs have helped me to live a good life, and have given me patience."

Religion is among her most important values. Others include family, friendships, and life. Raised by her single mother, grandmother, and an aunt; she was taught respect, obedience to elders, love of God, and how to deal with problems. She thinks it's important to teach her grandchildren how to cope with life, how to live a good life, and how to get along with others. She sees her role within the family as a "mother figure, advisor, and helper."

## Maria—Age 69

### Household Composition

| | |
|---|---|
| Husband | 67 |
| Son | 30 |
| Granddaughter | 32 |
| Great-grandson | 14 |
| Great-grandson | 11 |
| Great-grandson | 5 |

Maria is a 69-year-old great-grandmother who lives in a single-family home in Orange County, North Carolina. She is retired from cooking, and has a family income of approximately $17,500. Her sources of income are Social Security and retirement. She is a high school graduate. Maria has five children, eighteen grandchildren, and three great-grandchildren. She had her first child at age 16.

Maria takes care of her three great-grandchildren as well as her 67-year-old husband who has the beginnings of Alzheimer's Disease. Like most of the grandparents in the study, she is taking care of her great-grandchildren because of the persistent drug use of their mother who is in and out of the home. Her 32-year-old granddaughter, who is not financially able to support herself and her three sons, lives in Maria's home, as well as her 30-year-old son. Although Maria enjoys taking care of her great-grandchildren, the strain and stress of caregiving is wearing her down.

I feel good that they are safe, fed, and well taken care of. But, I am tired now. It's too much pressure. I cannot discipline them. They don't want to listen. Their mother aggravates the problem because she wants to control the house. I hope that I can stay healthy enough in body and mind to continue their caregiving.

Maria has a kind heart and a giving spirit. She speaks readily about caring for others, and the importance of teaching her grandchildren to help others.

Maria is burdened by the lack of support she receives from her immediate family. The household family members, including the husband, son, and granddaughter, all conspire against Maria. She is troubled and distressed about the way they treat her. "They want me to leave," she says. She thinks they deliberately try to make her life miserable. She receives no financial support from either the son or granddaughter to support the operation of the household. She speaks of the many years of psychological abuse from her husband.

Almost all married grandmothers in the study had experienced years of psychological abuse from their husbands. And many of those who were divorced, said that they left their husbands because of extreme physical and/or psychological abuse, and womanizing. Although physical abuse was not uncommon among the grandmothers in this sample, the majority of the reported abuse was psychological. Although her family support is weak, she is consoled by her spiritual relationships and involvement. She is a church member and attends church services and other activities regularly. She says that she receives most of her emotional support from her relationship with God, "I read the Bible and pray, I would not be able to do it without God."

In addition to her strong religious values, others include love, work, unity, relaxation, peace of mind, trust, respect, and caring for others. She was raised by her parents who taught her the importance of working hard, respecting elders, helping others, self-respect, love, responsibility, respect for history, and a healthy diet. She thinks it's important to teach her great-grandchildren to rely on self, respect others, reach for high goals beyond education, become fearless, know where you want to go, and know yourself. Maria sees her role as "the glue. I hold the family together," she says.

## Rose—Age 63

### Household Composition

| | |
|---|---|
| Husband | 65 |
| Daughter | 27 |
| Daughter | 31 |
| Son-in-law | 29 |
| Son-in-law | 32 |
| Granddaughter | 5 |
| Granddaughter | 3 |

Rose is a 63-year-old grandmother who has lived all of her life in rural Orange County, North Carolina. She shares a mobile home with her husband, two adopted daughters and their families. The small home is neatly adorned from wall to wall with family photos. She is retired, but worked in housekeeping at a local hospital for most of her adult life. She reports a household income of more than $40,000 from earnings, Social Security, and retirement.

Rose has taken care of her grandchildren for two years because their parents need to work, and other financial reasons. She says "there is nothing difficult about taking care of my grandchildren, I love having them around." Rose lives in a close-knit community consisting of mainly family members and longtime friends. In addition to the support she receives from her well-functioning extended family, she gets emotional as well as social support from other family members who share the family compound. This small rural community has all of the characteristics of a traditional African American family, where family and close friends share a special bond, there is mutual cooperation and support, and community members live by traditional black family values. Teenagers are involved in wholesome activities such as fishing or sitting around at the black-owned corner grocery store. They care about each other and are concerned about the welfare and survival of the community. This is truly a unique community.

Rose has the inner strength, self-reliance, and independence of our foremothers. She relies on God for most of her emotional support. She says, "I don't need much emotional support, because I don't get upset." In addition to her strong religious values, Rose loves her family. Raised by her parents, she was taught to be good to others, obey and respect the elderly, and work hard. She believes it's important to teach her grandchildren to stay in school, get a good education, believe in God, and stay drug free. Rose describes herself as an "advisor" and "supporter." "They all come to me. They all depend on me for financial, social, and emotional support."

## Willie Mae—Age 77

### Household Composition

| | |
|---|---|
| Daughter | 47 |
| Son | 44 |
| Daughter | 42 |
| Granddaughter | 10 |
| Grandson | 5 |

Willie Mae is a 77-year-old grandmother who lives in her own home that she shares with her three grown children and two grandchildren. She is a high-school dropout who has worked for most of her adult life as a cook and laundress. She reports an annual household income of more than

$40,000. This includes the earnings from the three adults in the household, Social Security, and a retirement pension. She has nine children and twenty-one grandchildren. She had her first child at age 17.

Willie Mae has taken care of her grandchildren since their birth, because their parents need to work. Although the children's parents live in the home, the grandmother takes on full responsibility for the care and well-being of the children. In spite of her advanced age, poor health, and obesity, she continues to prepare food and manage the home, seemingly, without much concern from her grown children. She does, however, get a lot of emotional and social support from her family.

This is a type of social structure where grown children do not leave home. It is clear, however, that this type of arrangement is very functional and free of conflict. The grandmother enjoys continuing her traditional role responsibilities. The home is filled with love, respect, and protection for the grandmother. Willie Mae feels good about taking care of her grandchildren. She says, "I've been doing it so long, it does not bother me." However, she is concerned about the need for after school care, respite care, and more financial support. She is concerned that she does not always have enough money for her medications.

Willie Mae was raised by her aunt who taught her many lifelong values. Religion, cleanliness, obedience, and the importance of knowing how to cook were learned early in her life. Her adult values include love of family, religion, togetherness, wealth, health, caring for others, and giving to others. The values that Willie Mae would like to instill in her grandchildren are love, religion, education, success, cleanliness, hard work, concern for others, respect, manners, and the ability to cook.

### Hazel—Age 65

#### Household Composition

| | |
|---|---|
| Daughter | 45 |
| Granddaughter | 13 |

Hazel is a 65-year-old grandmother who lives in an urban area of a North Carolina city. She completed high school as well as three years of college. She is retired and has worked for most of her adult life as a security officer. Her annual income is about $16,000 from retirement and Social Security. She has six children and seven grandchildren.

Hazel, stressed out from worry, has taken care of her 13-year-old granddaughter since shortly after birth, because of the drug and alcohol abuse and incarceration of the child's mother. "My daughter brought the baby to me when she was 2 months old. She has three other children that she gave away," says the mother. In spite of her multiple chronic health problems, for seven years, she has also taken care of her 45-year-old daughter who has emotional and mental problems, resulting from "taking drugs," says Hazel. When asked how she feels about being a grandparent caregiver at this point in her life she responds,

If I had to do it all over again, I would not. I'm concerned about not being able to handle her because I'm older. I can't take her places, and I'm not able to afford many things that I'd like. I'm also concerned about her education and discipline. She's getting suspended from school too much. She's very intelligent. She has been out of school for five days for threatening a girl. She needs to be in a Big Sister program. She needs discipline.

What Hazel is describing is an out-of-control teen with disciplinary problems and the grandmother does not know what to do. The teen has little respect for her grandmother. This situation is not uncommon among grandmothers who are raising teenagers. Grandmothers in this study, particularly those whose health is bad, are not able to deal with their high-energy teenage grandchildren. Hazel says that she is not mentally or physically able to take care of her granddaughter. She says that her mental health has deteriorated since she began caring for her granddaughter and her mentally disturbed daughter. This is clearly a situation where the grandmother can provide a home for her 13-year-old grandchild, but is unable to adequately supervise and raise her.

Hazel relies on her son and daughter, who do not live in the home, for the bulk of her social support. She relies on God for her emotional support. "My beliefs help me to love my granddaughter, it gives me patience," she says. Her granddaughter receives little adult support and supervision. Hazel, who was raised by extended family including aunts and other relatives, was taught cleanliness, honesty, the importance of a good education, value in saving money, and the belief that she was just as good as others. Her values include family, shelter, and religion. She thinks it's important to teach her granddaughter the importance of religion, when to walk away, and when to speak. She describes her role as mother to everyone; "I am the matriarch," she says.

## Vera—Age 60

### Household Composition

| | | | |
|---|---|---|---|
| Male companion | 50 | Grandson | 12 |
| Daughter | 36 | Grandson | 10 |
| Daughter | 33 | Grandson | 7 |
| Grandson | 23 | Granddaughter | 6 |
| Granddaughter | 13 | Granddaughter | 5 |
| Granddaughter | 12 | | |

Vera is a 60-year-old blind grandmother who shares her four-bedroom low-income apartment with her companion, daughters, and grandchildren.

She is a sixth-grade dropout. Vera, who has been separated from her husband for a number of years, has lived in her present dwelling for thirty years. She has never worked outside the home. She has an annual household income of approximately $20,000 from disability, Work First, and earnings from other family members. She has seven children and fifteen grandchildren.

Vera has been taking care of her grandchildren for about fourteen years. Although she is totally blind, she provides general care for her grandchildren, with not much support from her two live-in daughters. Her social and emotional support is fragmented. Her family support is lacking and she relies heavily on God. She is a church member, but rarely attends church services. She says that her spiritual beliefs help her to teach her grandchildren better.

Vera does not think she has any problems. However, on my two separate five-hour visits, I made a number of observations. She is severely exploited by her two grown daughters who are using drugs, and a 23-year-old grandson, none of which have steady employment. No one seems to take responsibility for the care of the home, and minimal care of the children. She is equally exploited by a male companion who lives with her under the guise of protecting her welfare. In addition to these social problems, she has a number of physical health problems including arthritis, glaucoma, problems breathing, hypertension, heart problems, circulation problems, and diabetes. To say the least, Vera is in a unique position as a grandmother caregiver. Ironically, even in cases where the grandmother is old, frail, or sick; grown children still see them as problem solvers and way makers. Growing old and becoming sick did not seem to be a concern for many grown children in the study with respect to their parents.

Exploitation by grown children in the home was a common occurrence in the study. And, in cases where grown children lived in the home, grandmothers generally had more problems. They most often provided little support to the grandmother. Routinely, the grandmother treated them as if they were grandchildren or dependent children. The were usually not expected to be responsible.

Vera values helping others, and love of family. As a child, her parents taught her to love God, get a good education, be nice to others, and respect the elderly. She thinks it's important to teach her grandchildren to get a good education, love God, and obey grown-ups. She describes her role as the "matriarch, provider, advisor, supporter, and helper."

## Sarah—Age 63

### Household Composition

| | |
|---|---|
| Granddaughter | 10 |
| Sister | 45 |

Sarah, a 63-year-old divorced grandmother, lives in urban North Carolina, in a small two-bedroom apartment that she shares with her sister and granddaughter. She is a high school graduate with two years of college, and has worked for most of her life as a clinical secretary. She is retired, but had to return to work to support her granddaughter. She reports an annual household income of $25,000 from Social Security and Work First. She has four children and six grandchildren. She had her first child at 21.

Sarah has been taking care of her granddaughter for six years, because of the drug use of her parents. Initially, Sarah had mixed feelings about taking full responsibility for the care of her granddaughter, but "after taking time to prepare psychologically for the challenge," she concluded that it was in the best interest of the child. Sarah discusses the circumstances that led to assuming care of her granddaughter,

My granddaughter's parents were not married when she was conceived. Her father deserted her mother, and the mother was about to put her up for adoption. She was being shifted from place to place. I wanted to provide a stable life for her. She needed a family to care for her. I was not planning to do this at this time in my life. I have adjusted to her, and I feel good about it now. I enjoy sharing with her and doing things with her. There is power in raising children, because Black women have never had power outside the home. The power in the home is the only power she has known.

Although Sarah has adjusted to the challenge and likes to teach and train her granddaughter, her custodial responsibilities are not without problems. She is concerned that her time is limited, she does not have enough money, and she has no other life. "I can't go to plays or a movie and these are the things I like to do. I can't afford a baby sitter. In addition, I don't have a good support system," she says. Sarah is particularly distressed over her inability to have affordable housing, her failing health, her age, and her overall inadequate financial position.

Sarah's parents taught her love of family, religion, hard work, and discipline. Her own adult values include health, family, appearance, education, life, spirituality, self-esteem, and inner peace. She is teaching her granddaughter the importance of self-esteem, friendship, education, self-sufficiency, survival, and sharing. She sees her role as the "matriarch" and "spiritual teacher." She adds, "in general, I see myself as playing many roles within the extended family network: educator, guidance counselor, provider, role model, and mother without being a mother."

## Lane—Age 66

**Household Composition**

| | |
|---|---|
| Grandson | 12 |
| Grandson | 10 |
| Grandson | 2 |
| Grandson | 1 |

Lane is a 66-year-old grandmother who cares for her four grandsons, all brothers, ranging in age from 1 to 12. She is retired, has a twelfth-grade education, and has worked for most of her adult life as an operator supervisor. She reports an annual income of $30,000, that she receives from her retirement pension and Work First. She rents her old Victorian home located in downtown Sanford, North Carolina. She has three children and seven grandchildren.

Lane moved to Sanford from New York one year ago. She has had primary care of her four grandsons since their birth. Both parents have drug and alcohol problems, as well as emotional and mental difficulties. In describing her full-time role as a custodial caregiver, Lane says,

I have to do everything. There is never a free moment to do anything for myself. Both parents of the children are on drugs and are not married. They take no interest in their children. My health is not good. If I get sick, who will care for them? What would happen to them if something happens to me? I had to move from New York because my grandsons' mother would steal my things from my home. Both my son and her would bring friends over to stay in my basement apartment. I could not allow all of them to take advantage of me.

However, in spite of the drawbacks, she says, "I have no regrets. I wish it could be different. Sometimes, it gets hard. I need some help with cooking, washing, and cleaning. I wish I could send them home and relax sometimes. I never get a break."

She believes her grandchildren are getting the best possible care she can provide. "In general, they are doing well and that makes me happy," she says. However, there are financial and health problems that concern Lane. She needs child-care assistance, transportation, and respite care. She is bothered by arthritis, hypertension, and diabetes. As she cuddles her youngest grandson, and yells out to the others, she speaks of their health needs and her inability to pay for the services.

All four boys have problems resulting from the effects of drug use by their mother. The 1-year-old was in the hospital for two months after birth, and in the outpatient clinic for nine months. He also needs a circumcision, but I'll have to pay. Social Services said that it's optional surgery, and they are not required to pay. One has a hernia that needs to be removed.

Lane has no social support. She says there is no one that she can call on for help. Her own children provide no support on any level. She says, "my faith keeps me going."

Lane, who was raised by her step-grandmother, was taught independence, to think for yourself, depend on God, and don't wait for others to do for you. Her adult values include love of family, health, religion, and living a good life. She thinks it's important to teach her grandchildren independence, value of education and religion, and that it's possible to be in charge of their own lives. Lane describes her role as the "backbone" of the family.

## Cammie—Age 62

### Household Composition

| | |
|---|---|
| Husband | 84 |
| Son | 47 |
| Granddaughter | 23 |
| Great-grandson | 4 |
| Great-grandson | 2 |

Cammie is a strong and savvy great-grandmother who lives in a small community in rural Orange County, North Carolina. She is a retired domestic and Head Start teacher. Her annual household income is about $8,000 that she receives from Social Security, disability, and Work First.

Cammie is not only custodial caregiver for her two great-grandchildren, she cares for her 84-year-old husband who has Alzheimer's Disease and a 47-year-old alcoholic son. She cares for her great-grandchildren because their mother, her granddaughter who is in and out of the home, neglected their needs because of drug use. In addition, "she is very angry and shows signs of severe emotional problems requiring treatment," says Cammie. Although she raised her granddaughter from the age of 2, she seems very resentful of her grandmother. She has cared for the great-grandchildren since birth. Cammie is concerned that her granddaughter is unmarried and pregnant again with her third child, but she says that she is not willing to take care of another child.

Cammie's caregiving responsibilities and competing family demands are extreme in relation to most grandmothers in the study. In addition to the problems associated with the care of her Alzheimer's husband, her alcoholic son, and the needs of her great-grandchildren, Cammie is constantly burdened by her granddaughter's hostile attitude toward her, and her lack of involvement and interest concerning her own children.

Although she lives in the home most of the time, she makes no effort to care for her children. She gets up when she wants, and then watches television until it's time for her to go to work. She has the same routine everyday. She doesn't even speak to me unless it's absolutely necessary. I am afraid of her.

Although Cammie loves her granddaughter, she would like to see her leave the home because it would be better for the children. "She is in and out of the home, and that is not good for the children," she says. The granddaughter has problems of her own. Her mother is in prison, her father is an alcoholic, and she is now pregnant with her third out-of-wedlock child that she cannot afford. Her emotional problems are exacerbated by these issues. Repeatedly, the grandmother says that her granddaughter needs treatment.

The granddaughter's presence and her problems is an added burden for Cammie and her custodial roles. The great-grandchildren have their own heath, social, and emotional problems. The 4-year-old is hyperactive and obese, and she needs counseling and dietary information for him. However, she says that she is not eligible for assistance because she is not legal guardian. She is saddened that her granddaughter will not take care of her own children, but refuses to relinquish custody to her. The custodial care as well as competing family demands are stressful for Cammie, however, she says, "I will not have it any other way." She said that she did not want Social Services to place the children "somewhere I'd never see them again, it hurts more to see them in foster care than for me to take care of them."

Although many grandmothers in the study really did not want to take care of their grandchildren for an indefinite period of time, almost all of them shared Cammie's notion about not wanting them to be in foster care. They were not particularly happy about having their grandchildren and great-grandchildren forced onto them either by the parents or Social Services, they also did not want them to be wards of the state. Because of the love they have for their grandchildren, and devotion to family, most felt that the only alternative was for them to take them, with or without adequate financial support and other needed resources. In spite of the behavior of their parent, it is difficult for the women in this study to turn their backs on their grandchildren. Their enduring strength is shown in their unconditional love and caregiving.

Cammie has very little informal support. She relies on her faith to get her through the day; she says, "If I did not have God on my side, I would not be able to cope." She was raised by her parents, who taught her to get along with others, love others, take responsibility for yourself and others, and work hard to get what you want. She values life, strength, health, and family. She thinks it's important to teach her great-grandchildren to love others, obey the elderly, get a good education, listen, and learn right from wrong. Cammie is pleased that she is still able to take care of her great-grandchildren at her age. She sees her role as "sole supporter of the family. If I don't do it, nothing gets done. If they did not have me, I don't know what they would do."

## Angel—Age 65

### Household Composition

| | | | |
|---|---|---|---|
| Grandson | 13 | Grandson | 8 |
| Grandson | 12 | Grandson | 3 |
| Great-granddaughter | 11 | Grandson | 2 |
| Grandson | 10 | Grandson | 2 |
| Granddaughter | 10 | | |

Angel, a 65-year-old grandmother, shares her four-bedroom rented home with eight grandchildren and one great-grandchild, ranging in age from 2–13. She is widowed, retired, and has a tenth-grade education. She receives the bulk of her $7,000 annual income from Social Security and Work First.

A trend among the grandmothers in this study is that grandchildren come into their care and a very young age, and remain for an indefinite period of time. Angel has been custodial caregiver for seven of her grandchildren since their birth because of the drug use and incarceration of their 32-year-old mother. One child belongs to a 41-year-old daughter, who abuses drugs and alcohol. "She just gave her child to me," Angel said. It is not clear why this great-grandmother is taking care of the great-grandchild. The grandchildren have only weak relationships with their mothers, and no relationships with their fathers. Angel works well with all of the children and they hold her in high esteem.

Angel has legal guardianship of all nine children, and treats them as if they were her own. She is efficient and very organized. During the several occasions that I visited with the family, one would not know that nine young children lived in the home, because they were all so well-mannered. Although taking care of her grandchildren has cut her retirement short, she says she "enjoys taking care of them, they need me. I'd rather have them than let them go to the state." However, Angel is concerned about not having enough money to get them the things they need, not having enough time for herself, and not being able to attend church. In spite of these burdens, however, Angel adds, "I like to be needed, and I would not have it any other way." The welfare of the grandchildren was the primary reason that led the grandmothers in this study to assume responsibility for their grandchildren.

Unlike the majority of grandmothers in the study, Angel has mastered the art of getting the needed health, social, educational resources for her grandchildren. She is a full-time grandmother in the sense that everything she does is related to their health and well-being. She manages the family like a business. The house is immaculate. She enforces the important values, and each family member has chores, except for the 2-year-old twins. The children are well-mannered and orderly. She is very active in their lives, and does not miss their health and dental appointments. She meets with their teachers regularly. Angel is not a well-educated woman, but she is savvy, disciplined, energetic, and resourceful. Angel is truly the model grandmother. In spite of the fact that Angel has the youngest children of all the grandmothers, and the greatest number, she exemplifies true strength and endurance in the face of adversity. She is an excellent example of doing what one has to do to survive.

Angel was raised by her mother, who taught her values such as cooking, sewing, canning, respect for the elderly, and education. Her adult values include life, family, health, feeling good, self-respect, respect for the elderly, love, determination, self-discipline, self-love, order, organization, cleanliness, and education. The values she thinks are important to teach her grandchildren are self-discipline, self-love, and determination. She wants her grandchildren to know that "they can achieve what they set their minds to." Angel describes herself as the "supporter, everybody looks to me for everything."

### Hollie—Age 71

**Household Composition**

Grandson          12
Granddaughter      9

Hollie, a 71-year-old grandmother, grew up on a farm in rural North Carolina. She is widowed and shares the house she rents with her two grandchildren. She is an eleventh-grade dropout. Her annual income is about $10,000 from Social Security and Work First. She worked for most of her adult life as a domestic.

Hollie assumed care of her grandchildren because her daughter neglected their needs and abused drugs. "I did not want my grandchildren in foster care. I care about my grandchildren and I want to take care of them," she states. She also cares for a 2-year-old great-grandchild during the day while the parents are at work. Like most of the grandmothers in the study, Hollie does not have legal custody of her grandchildren. She hopes one day her daughter will reclaim them.

Hollie says she enjoys taking care of her grandchildren. "I need someone to care about, and I like to see them grow," she says. In spite of her willingness to care for her grandchildren, she has a number of problems related to her ability to adequately care for them. These include the need for financial support, discipline, and respite care. Her 12-year-old grandson will not listen to her, and he walks out of the house without her permission. Other problems include the need for mentoring, tutoring, and after-school and summer programs. She is distressed that she does not have any time to herself. Because of her age and declining health, she does not have the energy to keep up with them. Like most of the grandmothers in the study, she wonders what will happen to her grandchildren when she is no longer able to care for them.

Hollie's problems are made worse by her willingness to allow her grown children to take advantage of her. She complains that her 40-year-old daughter, whose children she cares for, routinely drops off her weekly laundry and expects it to be washed, pressed, and folded the next day. One wonders where love ends and abuse begins. The abuse that many of these women experience from their children is among the sensitive issues that don't get addressed in the literature or in community settings. Many grandmothers become enablers, and inadvertently teach their children dependence instead of independence, a highly respected value in the African American culture.

Hollie, unlike most of the grandmothers in the study, has a healthy social support network of individuals she can depend on for help. However, she depends only on God when she feels depressed. "If I did not have God, I would not be able to do it," she says. She values giving, caring for others, family, and making others happy. Her parents taught her to believe in God, save money, stop complaining, and discipline. She wants her grandchildren to believe in God, get along with others, respect the elderly, and respect themselves. She describes her role within the family as the "backbone. Everyone comes to me when they want a caretaker."

## Mary—Age 88

### Household Composition

| | |
|---|---|
| Nephew | 66 |
| Granddaughter | 45 |
| Great-grandson | 25 |
| Great-great-grandson | 13 |
| Great-great-granddaughter | 10 |

Mary is an 88-year-old widowed great-great-grandmother who grew up in rural South Carolina, where she worked in the fields as a young child. She is a high school graduate and owns her old large home located in urban North Carolina. She has an annual income of $30,000 from employment, Social Security, and retirement.

Mary has cared for everyone in the household since their birth or shortly thereafter. Her 66-year-old nephew has lived with her for most of his life. Her 45-year-old granddaughter, who has AIDS, has never had her own residence. After her 25-year-old great-grandson was born, she assumed care for him, and later his two children. Mary enjoys raising children. She has raised her own children, grandchildren, great-grandchildren, great-great-grandchildren, nieces, nephews, and unrelated individuals for a total of forty-four years. She has raised eighteen nieces and nephews. "I enjoy raising children, this is my life, this is what I like to do, and this is what I do best," she says. And, although she is the oldest grandmother in the sample, she is among the 1 percent who reporting not being overwhelmed by responsibility. She also has the least number of physical health problems. She sees child care as a way of life, and not as an obligation or burden.

She makes raising children seem so easy. She says, "there is nothing difficult about raising children. When you love children, nothing is hard." She is not burdened by financial problems or lack of social support; nor is she consumed by the day-to-day child care responsibilities. She is concerned, however, with the question, "who will take care of the children when I die?" She has an adequate support network for getting things done like errands and chores. However, when it comes to emotional support, her support system either breaks down, or she refuses to ask. "Except for God and myself, there is no one else I can depend on," she says. Grandmothers in the sample generally reported that if they had God in their lives, they did not need anyone else. This is a reflection of the strong spiritual foundation and the rich love of God these elderly African American women experience in their daily lives.

Mary values family and religion. Her parents taught her the importance of religion, hard work, education, and how to cook and clean. She would like to see her great-great-grandchildren "grow up and be something, study hard and learn, and believe in God." She describes herself as "spiritual leader."

## Bonnie—Age 39

### Household Composition

| | |
|---|---|
| Daughter | 20 |
| Son | 17 |
| Son | 10 |
| Son | 8 |

Bonnie is a divorced, high school graduate who rents an apartment in a low-income housing complex. She shares a small cramped three-bedroom apartment with a daughter, who is the mother of her grandchild, three young sons, and her granddaughter. Presently, she is unemployed but looking for work. She was recently fired from her job because of conflicts between her child care duties and her job. She reports that she has held different types of jobs but has worked for most of her adult life in food service and city bus driving. For the previous year prior to this interview, she had an annual income of $20,000. Her only financial assistance comes from family members.

Bonnie takes care of her granddaughter because her 20-year-old daughter cannot afford her own place and is not willing to take care of herself and her young child. She says that she enjoys taking care of her granddaughter, but her joys are coupled with stresses. Although the baby's mother lives in the home, Bonnie receives no assistance of any kind to help take care of the child. Nor, does she receive any formal financial assistance for taking care of her granddaughter. When asked if she had contacted Family and Children Services for support, she replies, "No, I do not want them in my business." This attitude among grandparent caregivers is not unusual, particularly among grandmothers who have a history of being employed. The pain of distress, sadness, and despair is obvious. "Without a job, I don't know how I will provide for my family."

Bonnie receives most of her social and emotional support from her mother and 20-year-old custodial daughter whose child is in her care. She is a church member and attends church services weekly. She says that her spiritual beliefs have helped her take care of her granddaughter as well as her own minor children. "I think my spiritual beliefs have made me a better person, and have given me more patience," she says. Her church does not provide any assistance of any kind for the support and care of her grandchild.

Bonnie, who was raised in rural and urban North Carolina by her parents, was taught to serve God, love family, provide for yourself, respect the elderly, help others, and be responsible. Her own values include love for her family, happiness, religion, kindness to others, and helping others. She thinks its important to teach her children and grandchildren to love God and respect others. Bonnie sees her grandparenting role as "advisor, financial provider, problem solver, way maker, and counselor." She adds, "they look to me for everything."

## Betsy—Age 38

### Household Composition

| | |
|---|---|
| Companion | 40 |
| Son | 22 |
| Son | 21 |
| Daughter | 16 |
| Daughter | 14 |
| Granddaughter | 1 |

Betsy, a 38-year-old grandmother and the youngest in the sample, lives in a three-bedroom rented apartment in a low-income neighborhood with her two sons, two daughters, male companion, and granddaughter. She is a high school graduate and does catering for a living. She is employed full-time and reports a household income of more than $40,000. She has four children and one grandchild.

Betsy has taken care of her 1-year-old grandchild for seven months, and the child care arrangement is permanent. She intends to take care of both her grandchild and the child's father. Betsy takes care of her granddaughter because her mother is a teenager and cannot provide for her. She says that she enjoys taking care of her grandchild because it allows her to have quality time with her. However, her love for taking care of her grandchild does not eradicate the problems and burdens that go along with child care. Since she is employed full-time and attending school, there is ongoing conflict between work, child-care responsibilities, and school. She says, "child care is very demanding and I want to continue to be healthy and stable enough to take care of my grandchild." Betsy was not very happy at first about caring for her grandchild, but now she has adjusted and enjoys being a grandmother caregiver.

Betsy, independent and very private, considers herself the matriarch of her extended family, and works hard to keep the family close. Unlike many of the grandparents in the study, Betsy has a good support network of family and friends. Her strongest support comes from her live-in companion and her aunt. She gets along well with her son, the grandchild's father who lives in the home, as well as the teenage mother who comes to visit daily. She attends church services weekly, but like most grandmothers in the study, receives only social and emotional support from her church. "My spiritual beliefs have helped me by giving me patience to deal with my grandchild."

Betsy, who was raised by her mother in small town North Carolina, was taught discipline and independence, "which have been my strongest survival tools," she says. As a child, she also learned to respect the values of others, praise others, and to stand up for herself. Her own values as an adult, do not differ much from those she was taught as a child. Education, helping others, and respect are her most important values. She thinks it is important to teach her grandchild to respect others, get a good education, learn to be independent, and be all that she can be.

Although Betsy is young, strong, and energetic, she says that she feels overwhelmed by responsibility, a sentiment expressed my most of the grandmothers in the study. When asked, how she views her role within the family, she responds: "I am the matriarch, king, queen, supporter, role model, mother, sister, and brother."

### Lora—Age 39

**Household Composition**

| | |
|---|---|
| Daughter | 17 |
| Granddaughter | 2 |

Lora is a 39-year-old, never-married grandmother with a tenth-grade education. She lives in a poor, drug-infested, crime-ridden, inner-city neighborhood in Durham, North Carolina with her 17-year-old teenage daughter and 2-year-old granddaughter. She is employed part-time and had an annual income of approximately $12,000 in 1999. Her part-time earnings are supplemented by Work First (Aid to Families with Dependent Children) that she receives for her grandchild.

Lora assumed primary care for her 2-year-old granddaughter because the child's mother was only 15 years old when the grandchild was born and "unable and unwilling to care for her child," says Lora. The child's father is incarcerated. The grandmother is not very happy about taking care of her daughter and grandchild. "I want to help her out, but I also want her to get her own place," she says. Lora's need for day care is among her most pressing problems concerning the needs of her grandchild. Her own problems and needs, however, overshadow those of her grandchild.

Lora, mother of four of her own out-of-wedlock children, cried often during the interview and insisted of talking about her past. She stated that she has been on different types of mind-altering drugs since she was 24. However, she says that she has been clean for one month. On the day of our visit, she was anxiously awaiting the results of an AIDS test. She did not seem very optimistic.

Although generally upbeat, but distressed during the interview, her demeanor turned sorrowful when she spoke of her alcoholic mother, "who was never a real mother to me," she says. Her father died when she was 3, and she could not remember anything much from her mother's teachings. "Most of what I learned was from women in the streets." Lora's problems are centered around her own need for mental health care. She cried for most of the interview and stated that she felt depressed and overwhelmed by responsibility.

Similar to most grandmothers in the sample, Lora relies on God to deal with her stress. Unlike most grandparents, however, she does not attend church services. "God helps me get through the day," she says. In addition to the importance she places on God, she also values financial security, success, and goal-setting; all of the things she has not yet managed to achieve. She said that she learned cleaning and cooking from women in the streets. And, again, she refers to her mother's lack of involvement in her life; "my mother did not teach me much because she was an alcoholic," she reiterates. When asked what she thinks is important to teach her grandchild, she responds, "I think it's important to teach my grandchild the value of a good education and good manners." This young grandmother describes herself as a "caring mother, caretaker, and leader."

## Lenora—Age 48

### Household Composition

| | |
|---|---|
| Grandson | 15 |
| Grandson | 7 |
| Granddaughter | 12 |
| Granddaughter | 7 |

Lenora is a 48-year-old grandmother with a seventh-grade education. She rents an apartment that she shares with her four grandchildren. She has an approximate income of $15,000 and is not presently employed. She has worked in maintenance for most of her adult life. Her income comes primarily from Social Security benefits, Social Security Supplement, and Work First. She has three children and six grandchildren. Lenora's first child was born when she was 14, not unlike many of the grandmothers in the study.

Lenora has taken care of her four grandchildren, ages 7–15, from a very young age. There are multiple reasons why she is serving as primary caregiver. Among these are neglect, parents abuse of drugs and alcohol, emotional and mental problems of the mother as well as AIDS, and the incarceration of both parents.

The situation for some African American grandmothers is particularly devastating. Lenora's case was among the most grim. When asked why had she assumed the care of her grandchildren, she said,

The children's parents were out in the streets and were not taking care of the children. I want to provide them with stability, so I took them out of the shelter. The children were being sexually abused for money by my daughters and my daughters' father. My 2-year-old grandson has AIDS. I feel good that they are safe. I want them to be as normal as possible. My grands are my life.

These African American grandmothers are enthusiastic about taking care of their grandchildren, although many do not have the financial resources, formal support, or energy needed to carry out the tasks. Lenora is pleased that she can take care of her grandchildren, but she has some basic needs and concerns. She did not have a refrigerator that worked or a washing machine. She also needed furniture. She worries about the quality of her grandchildren's education. In spite of her needs, however, it was clear that she loves her grandchildren and feels good that they are safe.

In spite of the desperate situations of the grandmothers in the sample, they all had commendable values. Lenora was raised by her father who taught her the importance of family ties, religion, and survival. Her own values include education, religion, and family. She thinks it is important to teach her grandchildren to love one another. When asked, how she viewed her role within the family, Lenora responded, "I am the glue."

### Daisy—Age 48

**Household Composition**

| | |
|---|---|
| Husband | 54 |
| Grandson | 7 |
| Granddaughter | 10 |

Daisy is a 48-year-old grandmother who lives with her husband and two grandchildren in their own home. She completed high school and one year of college. She works full-time in the banking industry and earns more than $40,000 annually. She has one child and two grandchildren. Her only child was born when she was 19. The grandmothers in this study ranged in age from 14 to 19 when they had their first child.

Daisy has been primary caregiver for her granddaughter since birth, and has taken care of her 10-year-old granddaughter for seven years. When asked what lead to her decision to take care of her grandchildren, she responds:

They were living in poor conditions. My 26-year-old daughter could not take care of the children well. There was a lot of stress and pressure on her, and she had problems taking care of my sick granddaughter who is retarded. Their mother is not financially able to take care of the children, and I did not want them to be neglected.

Her concern for her grandchildren is similar to many grandmothers in the study who feel that they can do a better job of raising their grandchildren than their daughters. They also feel strongly about giving their grandchildren the opportunities, safe environments, and supports they gave their own children.

Daisy enjoys raising her grandchildren, "but I'd like it more if I did not have total responsibility," she says. "I could be a better grandmother, if I did not have to be a parent," she adds. Daisy speaks in desperation about her child care problems and the lack of support she receives from her husband. Her problems are centered around her need for respite care, her granddaughter's retardation, and coping with the stress of it all. Her 10-year-old granddaughter, takes eighteen different pills a day, she has seizures and two different brain disorders. She says, "sometimes, I get real tired and want to scream." She experiences difficulty getting the children ready for school in the mornings and picking them up from school, because it conflicts with her job responsibilities. She admits that taking care of her grandchildren has caused her to be depressed. She started depression medication since she started caring for her grandchildren. Again, she mentions the lack of support she receives from her husband. Many grandfathers in the study were very helpful to their spouses, especially those whose marital relationships were good. In cases where the marital relationships were bad, grandfathers made no effort to assist the grandmother with the care of the grandchildren. Although approximately 30 percent of the sample were married, the grandmothers, for the most part, took care of the grandchildren. However, many grandfathers were actively involved with their grandchildren and loved them very much. In spite of the problems, however, Daisy says, "it's good that I am able to do it. I regret that I cannot have the freedom I want. But, I feel that God will take me out of the situation when he sees fit."

Daisy was raised by her mother, who taught her many values for survival. Her family values include money, thrift, respect, proper behavior, family, responsibility, religion, solitude, happiness, financial stability, hard work, help others, education, and do not look to others for approval.

Daisy views her role within the family as the "provider."

### Natalie—Age 47

#### Household Composition

| | |
|---|---|
| Grandson | 11 |
| Grandson | 10 |
| Granddaughter | 4 |
| Granddaughter | 4 |
| Grandson | 2 |

Natalie is a 47-year-old tenth-grade dropout who shares her rented two-bedroom low-income apartment with five of her grandchildren. Presently unemployed, she has worked for most of her adult life as a cook. She has an annual income of $4,000 which comes primarily from Work First. Natalie has three children and eleven grandchildren. She had her first child when she was 17.

Natalie has taken care of five grandchildren since their mother's incarceration twelve months ago. She nervously speaks of the circumstances that led to the incarceration of her daughter.

I've never taken care of my grandchildren full-time. This is not the way I want to spend my time. My daughter left home to go to the Seven Eleven to get a pizza and ended up robbing the place with her cousin. I feel obligated to take care of my grandchildren. I know that they are not mistreated. I want to do the right thing for them. I enjoy taking care of them.

She has a number of problems with her child-care responsibilities, her health, and the structural conditions of her apartment building. She complains of needing money and clothing for the children. She suffers from heart problems, hypertension, problems breathing, and has recently had surgery. She is concerned that she has no social support and no one to call for help.

Her health and child care problems are exacerbated by the structural conditions of the apartment and the apartment complex. The morning I visited Natalie, it was a 35-degree day in October and there was no heat in the unit. Three of her five young grandchildren were in the home, all sharing one small, cluttered room. There were no beds, only mattresses on the floor in each bedroom. The structural conditions of the unit were deplorable. In addition to the lack of heat on the day of our interview, there were several other problems observed. There was a water leak in the bathroom, which had soaked the bathroom floor and was causing the ceiling below to fall; there was a poor water supply—not adequate for a shower or bath; there was only one working electrical outlet—drop cords were used all over the unit; and Natalie said that there had been no natural gas in the entire complex since 1975. She said that she had made several attempts to contact the owner/manager but was unsuccessful. It was clear to me that this complex should have been condemned, yet it was inhabited by the most vulnerable populations. It was equally clear to me that this grandmother was under an enormous amount of stress. In her desperation, she says, "I worry a lot. I have no money. I'm depressed and my health is gone." Natalie's housing condition is far worse than those of other low-income housing units seen in this study.

Natalie was raised by her mother who taught her self-reliance, honesty, truth, and independence. Her own values include family and happiness. She wants to teach her grandchildren the importance of work and education. When asked, how she views her role within the family, she hesitates and then answers, "I'm that women in *Soul Food*, everyone comes to me to talk about their problems."

## June—Age 48

**Household Composition**

| | |
|---|---|
| Grandson | 13 |
| Granddaughter | 10 |
| Son | 25 |

June, a 48-year-old divorced grandmother, shares her home with her 13-year-old grandson, 10-year-old granddaughter, and a 25-year-old son. She is a high school graduate, and has worked in the textile factories for most of her adult life. Her income, approximately $35,000 annually, comes from her full-time employment and welfare payments to her grandchildren. She has two children and three grandchildren. She had her first child when she was 17.

June has been primary caregiver for her two grandchildren for all of their lives, because of consistent emotional problems and neglect by their mother, as well as poor living conditions. Her 10-year-old granddaughter has cancer, and she did not think her daughter was taking care of her well. Although taking care of her grandchildren is an added responsibility for June, she takes pride in knowing that they are safe and in good care. She says, "I feel good because I know they are being taken care of well. I know where they are and what they are doing. At first, it was very difficult, but I've gotten comfortable now. They still get on my nerves but I am fine, generally."

Custodial grandparenting has many blessings, but there are also burdens. June discusses the difficulties, obstacles, problems, and concerns involving the conflicts of child care and her personal and work schedule.

I have no social life and I have less motivation to care for myself. I have no freedom, and when I have to leave them, I feel guilty. I have to work too hard to take care of them. The demands of taking care of my 10-year-old granddaughter who has cancer, conflicts with my work. I'm concerned that I can't be home when they come from school. I'm having problems keeping up with my own health. I don't like having to spend most of my money on them instead of myself.

June could benefit from respite care, child care, financial support, and assistance in identifying appropriate after-school programs.

June was raised by her parents, but her values were heavily influenced by her grandmother. She was taught not to judge others, criticize others, hard work, cleanliness, religion, family, and education. Grandmother's values for her grandchildren include religion, education, and success.

June sees herself as being "everything to everybody—the maid."

### Renee—Age 40

**Household Composition**

| | |
|---|---|
| Son | 19 |
| Daughter | 11 |
| Granddaughter | 1 |

Renee, a 40-year-old, never-married grandmother, grew up in Orange County, North Carolina. She has been renting in a low-income housing complex for the past nineteen years. She works full-time as a cook and has an eighth-grade education. She has four children and four grandchildren.

Renee takes care of her grandchild, and her son who is the father of the child, because they cannot afford a place of their own. Although taking care of her granddaughter puts a financial strain on her, Renee says that she enjoys taking care of her. "I am happy knowing that I can help someone," she says. She reports no real problems centered around her role as a primary caregiver, however she adds, "I could use some financial assistance." Although the need is often clear, many African American grandmothers hesitate to say they are in need of financial assistance, particularly those who are not receiving formal assistance from the state.

Renee has an adequate network of close friends and family. Although she is a church member, she says that she does not attend church services. However, she says that "my spiritual beliefs have helped me to get through the day." Along with her spiritual values, Renee believes in honesty, respect for elders, family, and hard work. These were the values taught to her by her parents, and she would like to teach them to her grandchild. She sees her role within the family as the "banker."

### Tammy—Age 45

**Household Composition**

| | |
|---|---|
| Husband | 49 |
| Daughter | 25 |
| Granddaughter | 5 |

Tammy lives with her husband, daughter, and granddaughter in suburban Durham, North Carolina. She is a high school graduate with two years of college. She is employed full-time as a teaching assistant. She reports an annual household income of more than $40,000 resulting from earnings. She and her husband own the home they have occupied for one year. She has two children and one grandchild. She had her first child when she was 19.

Tammy has taken care of her grandchild since her birth. When she assumed care of her granddaughter, the baby's mother, who lives in the home, was 20 years old—not a teenager as some are when grandmothers assume care. Nor were there any of the typical reasons for custodial care. When questioned about the circumstances that led to assuming the care of her grandchild, Tammy responds,

I wanted to spend time with my grandchild and make sure she was taken care of well. My daughter is not ready for the responsibility. I wanted to make sure she had a stable environment. My granddaughter is a lot of support for me. She keeps me in a good mood.

Tammy, like many of the grandmothers in the study, gets support from her grandchild. Assuming care of their grandchildren satisfies these women's need to nurture. Unlike many of the grandmothers in the study, however, Tammy has no problems or concerns regarding her caregiving duties. Her only concern is that there are no children in the neighborhood with whom her granddaughter can play. Her only concern for herself is the lack of private time.

Tammy and her granddaughter receive a lot of support from each other. The grandchild also receives a lot of support from her own mother who resides in the home. Tammy says, "they act like sisters" referring to the grandchild and her mother. Tammy gets little or no assistance from her daughter with the day-to-day responsibilities of taking care of her own child. She says, "I am concerned about the lack of involvement of my daughter in the life of her child. I do everything for my granddaughter as if she was my own. Her mother lives here with me, but I care for her as if she did not live here."

Mothers who take full responsibility for the care of grandchildren when the mother is in the home, is not uncommon in these African American families. In these cases the mother of the child acts like a sibling to their own child, and both are treated by the grandmother as her children. There many grandmothers in the sample who are enablers. In these cases, grandmothers are encouraging and enabling their children to be dependent and irresponsible adults who are rewarded for not taking responsibility for their children. This phenomenon needs further study.

Tammy was raised by her parents who taught her a number of values. Among these were self-confidence, self-respect, respect for others, education, open-mindedness, and to be nonjudgmental. Her own values include spirituality, family, health, communication, psychological well-being, education, time, and dependability. She thinks it's important to teach her granddaughter to respect others and herself. Tammy views her role within the family as "advisor" and "one who holds things together."

## Pamela—Age 45

### Household Composition

Granddaughter        10

Pamela is a 45-year-old grandmother who shares her low-income dwelling with her 10-year-old granddaughter. She is divorced, has an eighth-grade education, and has worked in food service and the tobacco industry for most of her adult life. She reports an annual income of slightly less than $7,000 from Social Security benefits. She has three children and three grandchildren.

Pamela has taken care of her granddaughter since birth because her mother, Pamela's daughter, was a teenage mother who abused drugs and alcohol and neglected the child's needs. She assumed care of the child after she was contacted by Social Services and learned that the mother was frequently seen in unhealthy environments with the child. The grandmother expresses her concerns:

I did not want my granddaughter to go to foster care, I felt like it was my obligation to take her, but it's difficult. My problems are discipline, lack of transportation, not having enough money, and not having enough time for myself.

The grandmother is hyperactive and is taking medication, which makes it more difficult for her to care for her grandchild. However, in spite of the problems and burdens, she says, "I have no regrets, she is like my own. We do a lot of things together, and I enjoy watching her grow."

Pamela does not get much support from family and friends. Like many grandmothers in the study, she relies on God and prayer. She says that her spiritual beliefs have "helped me to raise my children with love, teach them how to talk to others, and educate them to stay away from trouble." Similar to most of the grandmothers in the study, Pamela attends church regularly, but does not receive any type of support for the care of her grandchild. She receives much support from her 10-year-old grandchild, with whom she says she has a "great relationship." The grandmother reports that her granddaughter does not interact with her father, but has a wonderful relationship with her 25-year-old mother. The mother–daughter relationship is more like a sister–sister relationship, says the grandmother, "her mother is more like her sister than her mother. My granddaughter calls me mama and her mother Mary."

Raised by her mother, stepfather, and foster parents; she was taught to respect older people, work hard, take care of her property, love others, and believe in God. She values shelter, religion, and financial well-being. She wants to teach her granddaughter the importance of education, how to deal with others, and the difference between right and wrong. Having been an eighth-grade dropout, Pamela has high regards for education, she says, "education is life; we have to have it." She sees her role as a "spiritual leader."

## Nora—Age 49

### Household Composition

| | |
|---|---|
| Grandson | 14 |
| Granddaughter | 11 |
| Grandson | 7 |
| Brother | 50 |

Nora is a 49-year-old divorced grandmother who has cared for her three grandchildren since their birth. She also cares for her 50-year-old disabled brother. She is a high school graduate and has worked as a secretary for most of her adult life. Presently, she is not employed and not seeking work. Her $5,000 annual income comes primarily from Social Security benefits and Work First. She has three children and ten grandchildren.

Nora enjoys being a custodial grandparent to her three grandchildren whose mother is deceased. Her major problems are centered around discipline. "They want to have their way, and will not listen. They are getting into more trouble as they get older," she says. Although her health is good, like many grandparents in the study, she is concerned that as she gets older and more frail, she will not be able to care for her grandchildren. Her needs include transportation, clothing, and daily meals for herself.

Nora, like many of the grandmothers in the study, gets support from her grandchildren and has a good relationship with them. However, her informal social network in general is weak. She reports that she does not get help from any family member. She does, however, rely heavily on her religious beliefs. She is a church member and attends church service once a month. She says that her spiritual beliefs help her get through the day. "Prayer helps a lot with discipline, and provides inner peace and calm," she says.

In addition to religion, Nora's values include love of family, hard work, and wealth. Her parents raised her to love God, get a good education, work hard for what you want, and remain peaceful. She wants her grandchildren "to learn right from wrong, obedience, and good moral behavior." She views her role within the family as the "peacemaker."

## Inez—Age 48

### Household Composition

| | |
|---|---|
| Grandson | 8 |
| Granddaughter | 3 |

Inez is a 48-year-old divorced high school graduate who has taken care of her two grandchildren since their birth. She is a retired quality control inspector, with an approximate annual income of $20,000, which she receives from Social Security benefits and disability. She has two children and two grandchildren.

Inez is primary caregiver for her grandchildren because her daughter, their mother, neglected their needs and abused drugs and alcohol. She was a teen parent when her son was born. She enjoys the time she spends with her grandchildren. Although she says that she feels "great" about taking care of them, a number of problems and concerns are eminent.

I was not ready to take responsibility for grandchildren. I expected to have some grands at 60 or so. I never thought I'd live long enough to see my grandchildren. I can't take care of them like I want because I have health problems. It's hard trying to get involved in their social activities and helping them with their school work. Sometimes, I am not feeling well enough to take care of them.

Inez is concerned about not having health insurance for the children, as well as for her own health. She says, "I don't know what would happen to them if something happens to me. I don't think about myself, I think about everyone else."

Inez's social network is meager at best. She is a church member and attends services weekly. Her spiritual beliefs help her to teach her grandchildren better and help her to "stay focused." She has a fatalistic view of life, "whatever happens, we do not have control over it," she says. Inez's family support is particularly weak. Although she has good relationships with her grandchildren, she has a poor relationship with her daughter, the children's mother, who does not live in the home. In the following passage, she speaks of her daughter's lack of involvement in her children's lives:

I want her to be more stable, and take more responsibility toward her children. I want her to help with their care and welfare, spend more time with them, get involved with their school work, and be more involved in their lives in general. She loves her children, but she does not want the responsibility.

The grandchildren do not get very much support from either of their parents. They have accepted their grandmother as their primary caregiver.

Inez was raised by her parents who taught her a number of survival skills and values: religion, respect for elders, honesty, education, good moral behavior, no drinking or smoking, be home be sundown, and no entertainment or dancing (everything happened at church or school). Grandmother's values for her grandchildren included religion, honesty, respect for others, right from wrong, discipline, and education. Inez describes her role within the family in the following manner: boss, provider, inspiration to others, counselor, teacher, and doctor.

## Helen—Age 45

### Household Composition

| | |
|---|---|
| Sister | 35 |
| Daughter | 23 |
| Grandson | 4 |

Helen, a 45-year-old divorced grandmother rents the home that she shares with her daughter, sister, and grandson in inner-city Durham, North Carolina. She is a high school graduate, and employed as a retailer and inspector. She reports an annual household income of more than $40,000. She has two children and four grandchildren.

Helen is primary caregiver for her grandson because his mother, who lives in the home, needs to work. She says that she enjoys taking care of her grandson, and does not report any real problems or needs. Her only concern is that she would like to stay healthy and active enough to see him grow up.

Unlike most of the grandmothers in the study, Helen has an excellent relationship with her daughter, who lives in the home and is the mother of her grandchild. The grandchild also has a good relationship with his mother, as well as his father who does not live in the home. This grandmother also has a wealth of social support including a network of family and friends, unlike many of the grandmothers interviewed. She attends church regularly and participates in a number of church-related activities. She says that her spiritual beliefs give her strength and courage to love.

She has maintained traditional values, such as family, children, religion, and work. She also values friendship and health. Raised by her mother, Helen was taught the importance of leadership, survival, love, money sense, discipline, sharing, respect for the elderly, respect for children, and frugality. "Putting children first was very important to my mother," she says. She thinks it's important to teach her grandchild self-knowledge, assertion, to love, to respect others, and to share. "It's important for children to know and embrace their culture, and be able to connect the present to the past," she adds. This young grandmother see her role as a "leader, advisor, and financial supporter."

## Jennie—Age 45

### Household Composition

| | |
|---|---|
| Husband | 45 |
| Daughter | 29 |
| Daughter | 11 |
| Granddaughter | 4 |
| Grandson | 2 |

Jennie is a 45-year-old married grandmother who shares her low-income apartment with her disabled husband, two daughters, and two grandchildren. She is employed full-time as a housing authority counselor, but she has worked for most of her life as a nurse's aid. She has an annual household income of approximately $30,000 from employment and Work First. She has five children and four grandchildren.

Although Jennie is the primary caregiver for her two grandchildren, she gets assistance from the children's mother who lives in the home. The grandmother's primary role is to provide a place for them to live, meals, child care, and the bulk of the financial support. The children's mother is not employed and cannot afford a dwelling of her own. Jennie has been caring for the grandchildren for three years and the arrangement seems to be permanent. She also cares for her 45-year-old disabled husband. She enjoys her caregiving role because it allows her to develop a close bond with them. "I enjoy them referring to me as grandma," she says.

However, along with the blessings, there are also burdens. She says the "screaming and crying gets on my nerves at my age. Having to revisit child care after raising my own children is a real challenge for me." She is also concerned about not being able to give them "more material things." She would like to be able to do more for them. "My grandchildren need more financial assistance, and more recreational activities," says Jennie. In spite of the challenges, she says, "I really enjoy caring for my grandchildren."

Jennie receives strong social and emotional support from her church, but little from extended family members. She relies heavily on God and her minister. Her spiritual beliefs give her "peace of mind," she says. Like most of the grandmothers in the study, she is a church member and attends church services weekly. She is also involved in many church-related activities during the week. Jennie also gets additional support from her daughter, with whom she has an admirable relationship, as well as from her grandchildren, who show much love and respect. The children also share a loving relationship with their mother, although their father, who is not married to their mother, does not take an active role in their lives. "The children love their father, but he does not return their love. He has no sense of family and does not feel responsible for them," says Jennie.

Like most of the grandmothers in the study, Jennie loves her family and has a deep faith in God. She was raised by her mother and stepfather. As a child, her mother taught her how to cook. Her parents also taught her values, such as how to share, love, care, and respect others. As an adult she values family, peace of mind, food, health, money, God, love, transportation, and children. She wants to teach her grandchildren these values. Jennie describes herself as "head of the household and role model." She adds, "I take responsibility for everything."

## Laura—Age 46

### Household Composition

| | |
|---|---|
| Husband | 48 |
| Granddaughter | 12 |
| Grandson | 6 |

Laura, a 46-year-old grandmother, lives with her husband and two grandchildren in urban Durham, North Carolina. She is a high school graduate, is employed full-time in telecommunications, and reports a household income of more than $40,000. She has three children and five grandchildren.

Laura, who has taken care of her grandchildren for all of their lives, assumed care because of their mother's alcohol and drug use. She takes pride in caring for her grandchildren.

They are my children and I love to see them grow. But, this is not the way I'd hoped. The values we taught our children did not turn out the way we thought. I feel like I've been a parent for a long time. Everything happens for a reason.

The day I met with Laura, it was clear that she loved her grandchildren very much, but she was also very uneasy about having total responsibility for their care and well-being. Like most of the grandmothers in the study, she wanted to get out some of her emotions and spoke openly about her troubled relationship with her 30-year-old daughter, the children's mother. Our conversation was centered around her grandchildren, her daughter's drug use, and her nieces and nephews for whom she has assumed much responsibility.

Laura expressed a number of concerns regarding the care and welfare of her grandchildren. In addition to caring for the two grandchildren who live with her, Laura provides after-school care for two other grandchildren. Her child care responsibilities, along with her full-time job and failing health, leave Laura feeling overwhelmed. Like most grandmothers in the study, Laura spoke frankly about the drug and alcohol use of her daughter, whose children are in her care. She is concerned that her grandchildren will be influenced by their mother's drug use. Laura's 30-year-old daughter has been using drugs since her early twenties. She is distraught by this behavior, but feels helpless that she cannot do anything about it. Like many of the African American grandmothers in this study, she questions why the good values she taught her children did not work with her daughter.

She is also disturbed that her daughter does not share financial assistance that she receives from the state with her children. She does not want to report her daughter to Social Services or apply for guardianship because she does not want to deprive her daughter of her only means of financial survival. However, she is distressed that the money, instead of being used to take care of her children, is being used to help support her live-in mate. The daughter also has a 2-month-old child that Laura refuses to care for. She speaks of her daughter in less than cordial terms.

She spent their money this month, and I'm angry. It is a struggle. She is taking money from her children to buy drugs and support her man. I just go on and take care of my grandchildren. I try not to focus on the negative. I rationalize in order to get through the day. My hands are tied. I don't want to fight for custody, because her check will be cut off.

This grandmother's dilemma is caring for her grandchildren as well as her grown daughter.

But, her problems do not stop there. Laura's only sister died at age 40 leaving sixteen children, five under age 18. Laura took in the underage children and raised them as her own. She has "supervised, advised, and mothered" her nieces and nephews since her sister's death in 1969. Her responsibilities for the care and welfare of others are complicated by her declining health. Her muscles are weakening, but she has not been diagnosed with an illness. She is concerned that she will not stay healthy long enough to take care of her grandchildren until they are grown.

Laura is satisfied with her support, which comes from her spouse and a friend. She is a church member, but rarely attends church services. Her religious beliefs, however, are unwavering. She says that her belief in God has given her patience, wisdom, vision, and common sense. "I feel God sitting next to me and guiding me," she says. She receives support from, and has an excellent relationship with her grandchildren, she reports. However, the grandchildren do not get much support from either their mother or father, who live together. "The children love their mother, but there does not seem to be the mother–child bond between them. They rarely interact with their father. He does not want to be involved in their lives. He makes promises, but will not follow through."

Laura, who was raised by her mother, was taught to respect the elderly, help others, feed others, share with others, take care of family members, as well as the importance of education, independence, survival, home life, and health. These are the values she would like her grandchildren to live by. Laura sees her role as a "sparrow in a tree watching over them. I take responsibility for my family, my own children, and my nieces and nephews. I am their advisor."

### Julie—Age 47

**Household Composition**

| Grandson | 2 |
| Grandson | 4 |
| Grandson | 8 |

Julie, a 47-year-old grandmother with a high school education and three years of college, grew up in inner-city Durham, North Carolina. Julie, who has never been married, rents an apartment in a housing authority complex. She is employed full-time as a phlebotomist, making approximately $5,000 annually. She receives Work First assistance for her grandchildren to supplement her meager income.

Julie has been primary caregiver since the birth of all three children. The children were brought to her by Social Services because of the drug use and neglect by their 31-year-old mother. Although she is not pleased with the placement, Julie believes that her decision was in the best interest of the children. "I am concerned that I will have permanent responsibility for their care and well-being," said Julie. This grandmother is among the most vocal in her attitude of dislike for having to care for her grandchildren.

I truly love my grandchildren, but I never wanted to become a mother all over again. I feel that I have taken on more than I can bear at times. It's as if I have lost my life. If I had to make the choice to do it all over again, I don't think I would. This is not the way I planned my life at this point. I am very resentful that I am in this situation. I do not want to take care of my grandchildren. It has caused me to become depressed as well as put me in poverty. It's difficult to take care of a child with $72 a month. I feel torn between letting them go into foster care and keeping them. I don't want to take care of them, but I think it's my obligation.

Julie had become so outraged with her daughter, at one point during the interview, she said, "I hate my daughter for putting me in this situation." In spite of the frustrations, problems, and burdens, Julie is pleased that she is able to care for her grandchildren. Her emotional and social problems are aggravated by the need for financial assistance, respite care, after-school care, and summer programs. She is, by far, the most angry of all grandmothers who were dissatisfied with caring for their grandchildren. She adds, "I've sacrificed my career, gone into poverty, and ended up in public housing all because all because of the children. I've never had to live in public housing." Although she is the most outraged of all the grandmothers, she is also the most innovative, energetic, and industrious.

Julie's social support network is weak. She depends on one sister for assistance. But, for the most part, she relies on herself and God. She says that her faith has kept her going. "The scriptures calm me in the midst of problems, and Bible study has given me patience." In addition to religion, Julie values education, family, friends, shelter, safety, work, and life. Her mother taught her to be responsible and to get a good education. She thinks it's important to teach her grandchildren to respect others as well as oneself, love self which allows one to love others, get a good education in order to get a good job, have faith in the Almighty God, practice independence so as not to always depend on others, love freely, hate what is wrong and love what is right, dream big, set goals and carry them out.

She wants to teach them the importance of neatness and cleanliness and to always do right; don't do drugs, steal, or kill.

Julie sees her role within the family as a multifaceted one.

My role in the family is to be the caretaker, the maid, the mother, the father, and the grandmother. I'm the teacher, the nurse, the doctor, and most of all, the one to give them love and try to guide them in the right direction.

In an effort to show how stressful caregiving can be, Julie wrote the following essay called "Older and Returning to School." She talks about her struggles, her depression and lack of confidence; but eventually, with support, turns her life around to satisfy her needs. This is a beautifully written and wonderful story of how one grandmother turned her life around.

### Older and Returning to School: A Grandmother's Story

Being forced to take on the responsibility of raising my daughter's three children didn't quite seem to sit well with me. I'd had a hard enough time raising my own three children, and now that they are grown and on their own, I want to live my life doing some of the things that I have planned to do for myself. Taking on the responsibility of raising my three grandchildren, meant making some major changes in my life, changes that I didn't want to make. I didn't want to get up in the middle of the night to change baby diapers or have to fix formula or take the kids for doctors visits. Neither did I want the kids to go to Social Services to be placed in foster care or to be adopted by someone outside of my family. My daughter was on drugs and was not fit to take care of these three small kids. My family tries to help as much as possible, but they have their own families and problems.

In the year of 1999, I found myself at the lowest point of my life. There were times when I didn't know whether I wanted to live or die. Everything that I would do seemed to go wrong, even getting up in the morning was more that I wanted to bear. I wasn't the same person that I once was. Somehow, someplace I had lost the real me in the midst of my family and my own problems. I knew for the last past eight years I had been feeling somewhat depressed, but what I didn't know was how to get rid of those dark gray feelings that seemed to be taking over my life. It was like fighting a battle, and I wasn't winning. Now that I think about it, I don't believe I was trying very hard to win. I was just there because God wasn't ready for me at that time. There had to be a reason or some purpose that I was still here.

One morning I decided to go to Operation Breakthrough. I had heard from a friend that they were giving a program that I may be interested in taking. I thought I could get some help and information from other grandmothers in similar situations. Operation Breakthrough is a nonprofit organization that assists low-income people with child care and other continuing education programs. I was talking to one of the ladies there about my past jobs and experiences. I was telling here how I wanted to go back to work or back to school.

She asked me if I had heard about the Life Sufficiency Program given by The Salvation Army. She told me that the program was free, and that it was a good program. Her niece was enrolled there at the time. That very same day I called The Salvation Army to inquire more about the program. Knowing very little about The Salvation Army, I must say I had my doubts taking a class there. I thought The Salvation Army was a place where you could get food or clothing if your income was very low or you were out of a job. After talking to Candace, the Case Manager there, and finding out what the program had to offer, I decided to give it a try. August 25, 1999 I enrolled as a student in the Salvation Army Life Sufficiency Program. Since becoming a student here, my life has changed in more ways than one. When I came here, I was still very depressed, feeling down and out, and almost hopeless. I was feeling this way because I felt that my life as I planned it had been taken away from me and I didn't know where or how to start over. Now I can truly say, I feel good about myself and about my future.

Working with Candace, Marty, and Denise in the Life Management part of the program has made me realize that I can take back control of my life, my future, and set new goals for myself. JoAnn and Pamela of the Durham Literacy Council have been a joy to work with. Even though I have my high school diploma, they have made me realize just how much I have forgotten and how important it is to continue to learn. Last but not least, there is John the computer instructor. John has a way of making you want to learn more and more about computers. He makes learning fun. His patience and willingness to go out of his way to help each and every one of us has made me realize that I can reach the goals I set in my life.

Starting over again has got to be one of the most challenging tasks that I have ever had to endeavor. The feelings of uncertainty and the controversy within myself brought to mind the words of the great civil rights leader, Dr. Martin Luther King, Jr. and I quote, "the ultimate measure of a man is not where he stands in moments of comfort and convenience, but where he stands in times of challenge and controversy."

The Salvation Army Life Sufficiency Program has made me believe that I can stand on my own again. I can't get back to where I once was but I can start over. I have control of my life, I have set my goals, I will meet my goals, I can deal with stress, I can get a job, I can manage my money, I can fall and I will get back up, I will be rejected, and I will try again, I can, I will, I am self sufficient.

47-year-old Grandmother, Durham, North Carolina

### Sally—Age 52

**Household Composition**

Divorced husband     56
Grandson             15

Sally is a 52-year-old grandmother who has completed high school and two years of college. She is divorced and lives in her own home with her 15-year-old grandson and 56-year-old divorced husband. She is retired on disability and has worked for most of her adult life as a nursing assistant, clerk, and child-care provider. She reports an annual income of less than $5,000 which comes from Work First. She has two children and seven grandchildren. She had her first child when she was 17.

Sally has been primary caregiver for her grandson for less than one year. She is not at all pleased with her decision to assume care. She decided to care for him after learning that he was being neglected and physically abused by his mother. Sally has second thoughts, however, about being a grandparent caregiver at this time in her life.

It's something I have to do for my grandson. I've resented it because I feel that I've been forced to take on responsibility that's not mine. I don't like taking care of my grandson. He has discipline problems and is very angry that he has to live with me. He's trying hard to deal with the consequences of abuse by himself. It's difficult trying to get him to understand that all people are not bad. He needs anger-management counseling. I want him to get counseling and go back home. If he does not get counseling, I'm afraid that the streets will get him. Social Services is not supportive.

In addition to providing care for her 15-year-old grandson, Sally provides after-school care for two other grandchildren. "Child care is natural to me," she says. "I've taken care of children since I was four years old." Sally had responsibility for caring for her younger siblings while her parents worked. "I've known nothing but responsibility," she adds. Her child-care responsibilities are exacerbated by her terminal illness, caused by a rare bone disease, resulting in constant and severe pain. "I stay in pain, but I cover up my pain because I don't want my grandson to worry." She gets little support from her divorced husband who shares her home with her.

Sally was raised by her parents who taught her right from wrong, hard work, strength, spiritual love, and the importance of a clean soul. She wants to teach her grandson self-reliance, love, and forgiveness. When asked, how she views her role within the family, she responds, "They see me as the pillar of strength. Dependable. Everyone leans on me. They don't think I hurt. They don't think I have feelings. They act like I'm not human. They think I'll never die."

## Cora—Age 58

### Household Composition

| | |
|---|---|
| Husband | 58 |
| Daughter | 23 |
| Grandson | 8 |
| Granddaughter | 2 |

Cora is a 58-year-old married grandmother who lives in her own home with her husband, daughter, and two grandchildren. She is a high school graduate and works full-time as a housekeeping supervisor. She reports an annual household income of approximately $30,000. These earnings come from her employment, disability payments, and Work First. She has four children and six grandchildren.

Cora is primary caregiver for her two grandchildren, part-time caregiver for another grandchild, and she takes care of her sick husband. She assumed care of her grandchildren eight months prior to this interview, because of drug use and neglect from their parents, who are not married. She is concerned about her own health, and financial support for the children. When asked how she feels about being a grandparent caregiver at this point in her life, she responds,

I don't feel very good about it. I think I'm too old. They will not get everything they need. Many things they might need, I might not always be aware of, or have time to find out about. If I was retired, it would be OK. It's too much on me. I don't have time. I have a sick husband and it's too much.

Cora is troubled about the lack of activities and programs, as well as disciplinary problems concerning her grandchildren. Her grandchildren need more activities and programs, but Cora says that she does not have time to explore them because of her sick husband. She says that her 8-year-old grandson is acting out because he is not able to live with his mother. She is having disciplinary problems with him. She believes the grandchildren's problems are aggravated because of their interracial status. She thinks they feel rejected. She says, "they add joy to my life, but I would wish for them to be with their mother." The children do not get much support from their father, the grandmother's son, who is in and out of the home and on drugs. She speaks of the negative influence this might have on her grandchildren's future behavior. The children's mother visits with them weekly.

Cora expresses concerns for her grandchildren's future. She seems troubled about their potential for getting involved with drugs. She wants them to be able to go to college. "Will I be able to send them to college? Will I be able to raise them? Will my health hold up? Will I be strong enough or in tune enough to keep them out of drugs? These are among the many valid questions Cora has concerning her grandchildren's future.

Cora has a wealth of family and friends to help her and who give her instrumental support. However, like most of the grandmothers in the study, she relies on herself and God for her emotional support. She says, "I could not make it without faith." She is a church member and attends church services weekly. Raised by her parents in Orange County, North Carolina, she was taught many values for survival: religion, independence, work for what you want, respect for self and others, self-respect, trust, independence, religion, family health, and education. Grandmother's values for her grandchild include education, respect, responsibility, and religion. She sees her role within the family as the "sole supporter."

## Mae—Age 50

### Household Composition

| | |
|---|---|
| Granddaughter | 9 |
| Grandson | 2 |

Mae, a 50-year-old never- married grandmother, lives with her two grandchildren in a low-income rented housing in inner-city Durham, North Carolina. She dropped out of school after completing ninth grade, and has never been employed outside the home. She reports an annual household income of slightly less than $3,000 which comes from Work First only. She has one child and three grandchildren.

Mae has taken care of her son's children since their birth. She has also taken care of another grandchild part-time for thirteen of his fifteen years. She assumed full-time care of her grandchildren because their needs were not being met. They were neglected because their unwed parents—23-year-old mother and 36-year-old father—abused drugs and alcohol. Their mother was also a teenager when the children were born, and was not financially or emotionally able to care for the children. The children's father was legally blinded by gunshot pellets 13 years. The children were placed with Mae by Social Services. Mae does not have any regrets about taking care of her grandchildren. She thinks "it's great." She did not want her grandchildren to go to foster care. "I could not miss the joy of taking care of them; I love their hugs, kisses, and love," she says.

Like most of the grandparents in the study, Mae's social support network is weak, her support from family is meager, and she relies on herself and God for her emotional support. She is very spiritual and says, "my religious beliefs have give me hope and patience." She is a church member and attends services weekly. Although her support is generally weak, she gets good support from her grandchildren, who "enjoy the time they spend with me." The children receive little support from their parents, who are in and out of the home, and Mae receives no assistance from them for the care of their children.

Grandmother Mae was raised by her mother and grandparents. She was taught discipline and honesty. She values religion, doing her best, family, sacrifice, love, and caring for others. She wants to teach her grandchildren the importance of self-love, loving others, and education. Mae sees her role within the family as "spiritual leader." She says "Everyone acts like I'm their mother."

### Allison—Age 59

**Household Composition**

| | |
|---|---|
| Granddaughter | 10 |
| Granddaughter | 3 |

Allison is a 59-year-old divorced grandmother who lives in a rented apartment with her two granddaughters. She completed high school, is employed full-time, and has an annual income of approximately $7,000. She has worked for most of her adult life in the health care profession. She has six children and twenty-five grandchildren. She had her first child when she was 19.

Allison has been primary caregiver for her two young granddaughters for six months. The abuse of drugs and alcohol by the parents and their subsequent incarceration were the primary reasons for the grandmother assuming care of the grandchildren. "The children were shifted from one foster-care home to another, and I became concerned about the quality of their care," said Allison. Initially, she did not want primary care for her grandchildren, but when she visited them in foster care, she observed that their needs were not being met. She said that "they were worse off in foster care than with their parents. I wanted to provide a stable environment for them."

Allison has a number of financial, housing, educational, and health concerns. Her one-bedroom apartment is not adequate for three people. In addition, she is very dissatisfied with the public school system.

I don't have enough money to take care of my grandchildren. They need tutors and I need respite care. We need adequate and affordable housing. I want to help develop them into professionals, but the public school system is racist. I want to stay healthy in mind and body for my grandchildren.

Allison was raised by her aunt and uncle who taught her to be good, honest, get a good education, work hard for what you want, and love your family. She values family and security. She would like to teach her grandchildren to live by the Golden Rule. She views her role within the family as "the strong one" and the "enabler."

### Annie—Age 54

#### Household Composition

| | |
|---|---|
| Husband | 54 |
| Nephew | 41 |
| Grandson | 16 |
| Granddaughter | 11 |
| Granddaughter | 10 |
| Grandson | 10 |
| Grandson | 9 |
| Grandson | 9 |

Annie, a 54-year-old grandmother, lives with her husband, nephew, two granddaughters, and four grandsons in her large home in urban North Carolina. She completed high school and three years of college. She has worked for most of her adult life as a nurse. Her annual household income of approximately $30,000 comes from part-time earnings, Social Security, and Work First. She has three children and fourteen grandchildren. She had her first child when she was 19.

Annie has been primary caregiver for her grandchildren, ages 9–16, at various times for a total of twenty years. She enjoys the responsibility of caring for them. "I like seeing their different personalities. I like seeing them learn and grow. The keep me young," Annie says. She is concerned about staying healthy enough to get them through teenage years. Her grandchildren's needs include tutoring and a Big Brother program.

Annie was raised by her parents who taught her honesty, hard work, respect, and religious values. Her values include good morals, religion, honesty, and fairness. She would like teach her grandchildren love, fairness, honesty, kindness, hard work, respect, and the importance of education and religion. She sees her role within the family as "nurturer."

### Carrie—Age 51

#### Household Composition

| | |
|---|---|
| Granddaughter | 13 |
| Grandson | 8 |
| Companion | 50 |

Carrie, a 51-year-old grandmother, shares a rented low-income dwelling with her grandchildren and companion of thirty-five years. She is one of seventeen children raised by her parents in Durham, North Carolina. She dropped out of school after completing the eighth grade and has never worked outside the home. Her annual income of $5,300 comes from disability and Supplemental Social Security. She has five children and twenty-one grandchildren. Carrie, like most of the grandmothers in the study, had her first child as a teenager; her oldest was born when she was 15.

She has taken care of her grandchildren since birth, because of drug use and neglect by their parents, who are not married and do not live in the home. She also takes care of a third grandchild part-time because the parents need to work. Carrie takes care of her grandchildren as if they were her own. She says, "I feel good about raising them, I like having them around." She says that she has adjusted to most of the problems that come with being a unexpected grandparent caregiver. Her family support is good for instrumental tasks, but weak when it comes to emotional support. She relies on God and prayer.

Carrie was raised by her parents who taught her to respect elders, and offered words of wisdom such as mind your own business, don't get pregnant, and go to school. She values cleanliness and family. She's teaching her grandchildren right from wrong, honesty, and respect for the elderly. She sees her role within the family as "mother."

### Evelyn—Age 53

**Household Composition**

| | |
|---|---|
| Husband | 65 |
| Grandson | 12 |

Evelyn is a married 53-year-old grandmother, who lives with her husband and grandson in a single-family home in suburban Durham, North Carolina. She is a retired high school teacher who completed one year of graduate school. The annual family income is more than $40,000 which comes from Social Security benefits, disability, and earnings from her husband's religious ministry.

Evelyn has taken care of her grandson since his birth. Evelyn also takes care of her blind husband. Her own health is fragile. She is in the early stages of multiple sclerosis. She assumed care of her grandson because her daughter was a teenage parent. By the time, the mother was emotionally secure enough to care for her own child, the grandmother had become attached and did not want to release him. The arrangement became permanent with the daughter's blessings. She enjoys taking care of her grandson. Her only concern is "my grandson not knowing his father," she says.

Evelyn attends church often with her husband, but is not involved in church activities. She has a strong social network of family and friends. She receives strength from her husband and God. She values family and caring for others. Her parents taught her the importance of hard work, a good education, love, and cleanliness. She thinks it's important to teach her grandchild how to love. Evelyn sees her role within the family as the "mother, counselor, and friend."

### Beatrice—Age 54

**Household Composition**

| | |
|---|---|
| Granddaughter | 17 |
| Daughter-in-law | 37 |
| Son | 38 |
| Male companion | 48 |

"My spiritual beliefs keep me going," says 54-year-old Beatrice who is wheelchair-bound with a number of physical illnesses. She is a widowed, high school dropout, who has lived in a low-income housing authority complex for the past sixteen years. She is retired on disability and has an annual income of approximately $5,500. She has worked for most of her adult life as a nurse's aid. She has three children and three grandchildren.

Beatrice has taken care of her 17-year-old granddaughter for eight years. She also cares for two other grandchildren part-time. She provides full-time care because the parents neglected the grandchild's needs, and they all needed a place to stay. Although Beatrice has multiple illnesses and is wheelchair-bound because of obesity, she says that caring for her grandchildren is enjoyable and fun. "They are mine, and I love them," she says. The difficult aspect of child care "is not being able to work with them." She does, however, get to do a few things with them, such as watch television and help with their school work. She is limited in her mobility and interaction, but says, "I am grateful to have them in my care."

Beatrice's burdens are centered around her health and weak support system. She does not have a good relationship with her daughter-in-law who lives in the home. Although she is very ill, everyone looks to her for financial and spiritual support. She is a church member, but does not attend often because of her poor health. "Without my spiritual beliefs, I could not make it," she says.

Beatrice, who was raised by her grandfather, was taught to value religion, responsibility, self-reliance, and housework. Her own values do not vary much from those taught to her by her grandfather. These are self-respect, life, religion, and live by the Golden Rule. "I think it's important to teach my grandchildren to be respectful, value life, be responsible, and know right from wrong."

### Betty—Age 51

**Household Composition**

| | |
|---|---|
| Daughter | 23 |
| Grandson | 2 |
| Grandson | 5 months |

Betty, 51, cares for her daughter and her grandchildren, and lives in suburban Durham, North Carolina. She has master's degree and is employed full-time as a public health educator. Her annual household income is more than $40,000 which comes from earnings and Work First payments. She owns her own home as well as other real estate. She has two children and four grandchildren.

Betty takes care of her two grandchildren because their mother is attending school and needs to work. She enjoys taking care of her grandchildren because of the "unconditional love I get from them; at times it's the only thing that brings me joy," she says. Her role responsibilities have their problems, however. She says the role of grandparent caregiver "is coming a little sooner than I'd like." Since Betty works from home, her caregiving tasks make it more difficult for her to focus on her work. Her roles are exacerbated by her 23-year-old daughter's depression and refusal to seek treatment. Betty says, "I am stressed out from many things. I need more time for myself."

Like many of the grandparents in the study, this grandmother receives much of her social support from her grandchildren. She reports that she has an excellent relationship with the grandchildren, and a fair relationship with her daughter. The grandchildren have a good relationship with their mother, but there is no contact with either father. Betty also gets emotional and social support from her church. She states, "faith and prayer help me to cope. I stay focused on the principles of love, joy, and peace." Betty relies heavily on God when she is under stress, upset, or down-in-the dumps.

In addition to her faith in God, Betty believes in the importance of family, education, and racial unity. As a child, she was taught by her parents to believe in God, work hard, get a good education, help others, commit to family, respect others, as well as the importance of integrity and responsibility. She wants to teach her grandchildren to love God; maintain good morals; foster good self-esteem; develop self-confidence, imagination, and creativity; enjoy life; and be able to see beyond the obvious. She sees her role as "leader. I get things done," she says.

## Missie—Age 54

### Household Composition

| | |
|---|---|
| Granddaughter | 15 |
| Granddaughter | 14 |
| Grandson | 12 |
| Grandson | 7 |

Missie is a 54-year-old separated grandmother who was born and raised in Orange County, North Carolina. She is a tenant in a low-rent housing complex, that she shares with her four grandchildren. She is a high school graduate and has worked for most of her adult life as a secretary. Her annual income is approximately $5,000, which comes from part-time employment, regular assistance from family, and Work First. She has three children and ten grandchildren.

Missie is taking care of four grandchildren because their mothers are on drugs and neglected their needs. She assumed custodial care because she did not want her grandchildren to go into foster care. She is also part-time caregiver for another grandchild whose parents need to work. The role of custodial caregiver has presented a number of problems and concerns for Missie,

Two-hundred and seventy one dollars is not enough money to take care of my grandchildren. I had different plans for my life. I am not able to do the things I want to do, after raising my own children. I have to put what I want to do on the back burner. I am concerned about the health of my two grandsons (7 and 12) who have serious emotional problems. My 7-year-old grandson weighs only 47 pounds. I have to dress him for school and he cries every morning. I have to tell him everything he has to do, and he bothers other kids constantly. He runs through the house constantly. He has had emotional problems since birth. Both boys have a bad temper. Both have been taken to mental health. My health has gotten worse because of them. I feel helpless because I cannot get essentials for myself because of the expense for my grandchildren. I need a break.

Her problems and concerns are compounded by the problems associated with her teenage granddaughters behavior. Missie has multiple health problems, requiring her to take thirty-three different medications. She believes her health has gotten worse because of her grandchildren. However, in spite of her severe health problems, and the emotional and social problems of her grandchildren, Missie remains committed. She says, "they are mine and I love them. I want them to grow up and be healthy."

The grandchildren are loved by their grandmother, but have no relationship with their fathers. They don't respect their mothers, her daughters, the grandmother says. They see their mothers once or twice per week. "Both my daughters are in their thirties and on crack cocaine. One mother stole the children's Christmas gifts and sold them for crack. I love my children, but I can't do anything about their drug problem," she says.

Missie has very poor informal social support networks. When she feels upset or down-in-dumps, she calls the Crisis Hotline. She is not affiliated with a religious institution and does not attend a place of worship, however, she believes in "God who keeps me strong for my family," she says. In addition to family, she values health, home, and work. She parents taught her to respect elders, love God, and love one another. She thinks it's important to teach her grandchildren respect, good citizenship, responsibility, and to live by the Golden Rule. She sees her role within the family as "the rock." She says, "I'm the mom, dad, grandma, and the granddad. I do it all."

## Rachael—Age 54

### Household Composition

| | |
|---|---|
| Son | 31 |
| Grandson | 9 |
| Grandson | 6 |

Rachael, a 54-year-old separated grandmother, is head of household for her two grandsons and their father. She is a high school graduate and has worked for most of her adult life in food service. Her household income is slightly less than $15,000 annually. She rents the home where she has lived for five years. Her primary income sources are her earnings and Work First. She has three children and nine grandchildren.

Rachael has taken care of her 6-year-old grandson since birth, and her 9-year-old grandson for five years. She is raising her grandchildren, "because my daughters just don't want to raise their own children," she said. In addition to providing full-time care for two grandchildren, she also has also taken care of three great-grandchildren since their birth. Rachael says that she enjoys taking care of her grandchildren; "I like doing things for them." However, custodial grandparenting is not without its problems. "I have to plan all of my activities around them," she says. She complains that she does not receive enough financial support from their fathers. In addition, she says, "they need tutors, good summer programs, and mentoring. I need respite care." There are rewards as well as burdens. Rachael says, "caring for them keeps me out of trouble. It's meaningful." She takes care of her grandchildren "by choice," she boasts about proudly.

This grandmother has a number of individuals she depends on for help, and reports that she is very satisfied with their assistance. However, like most of the grandmothers in this study, her emotional support network is weak. She relies on herself, a sister, and God for her emotional support. She is a church member and attends services regularly. She says her church activities keep her "peaceful and involved." Like most of the grandmothers in the study, Rachael has a good relationship with her grandchildren. However, the children do not receive much support from either of their parents. The vast majority of grandchildren in this study are not involved in their fathers' lives, and many do not know the identity of their father.

Rachael was raised by her aunt who taught her the value of independence, education, hard work, and responsibility. She learned responsibility at an early age, because she had to care for six younger siblings. She values family, health, comfort, and financial well-being. She thinks it's important to teach her grandchildren to respect others, defend self, value independence, and have good manners. He describes herself as the "glue that holds the family together."

### Barbara—Age 51

**Household Composition**

Grandson        7

Barbara is a divorced 51-year-old grandmother who rents her home that she shares with her 7-year-old grandson. She is a high school graduate and has completed three years of college. She is employed full-time as a secretary, and reports an annual income of $30,000. She has three children and five grandchildren.

This grandmother assumed care of her grandson, resulting from an interracial relationship, after her son's teenage girlfriend gave him up for adoption. Although the mother knows that her child is with the grandmother, she has made no effort to see the child, says the grandmother. She has not spoken with him since he began to talk, five years ago. The child's father also has a poor relationship with his son. The grandmother says that she has a wonderful relationship with her grandson.

She enjoys taking care of her grandchild, but there are problems. "We do everything together. At first, adjustment was hard, but it's fine now." She had raised her own children and did not want to start all over again. A big concern for Barbara is that her grandson gets very angry about being with her, although she says he has gotten better with age. She has concerns about her own health. In addition to her health problems, she admits to being overweight, and is not sure of how long she will be able to care for her grandson. Like many grandmothers, she agonizes over what would happen to her grandson is she is no longer able to care for him.

Barbara reports that she is very satisfied with her support network of family and friends. However, she relies primarily on a daughter and her mother. Although she says that she is not very involved in church activities, she attends church services regularly, and says that her spiritual beliefs have helped a lot in caring for her grandson. Her spirituality gives her "peace of mind and a better attitude about being a custodial caregiver," she says. Religion is only one of the values that have maintained Barbara over the years. Others include respect, good communication, honesty, and helping others. As a child, Barbara was taught to respect authority, and believe in God. She thinks it's important to teach her grandson to be respectful, and believe in the Golden Rule, be nice but hold your ground, value independence, learn to deal with criticism, and learn to deal with peer pressure. Barbara sees her role in the family as "advisor, educator, and a source of wisdom."

## Dottie—Age 59

### Household Composition

| | |
|---|---|
| Daughter | 43 |
| Grandson | 12 |
| Grandson | 11 |
| Grandson | 11 |
| Granddaughter | 9 |
| Grandson | 7 |
| Grandson | 6 |
| Grandson | 6 |

Dottie, a 59-year-old divorced grandmother lives in a small, crowded house in Durham, North Carolina. She has an eleventh-grade education, and retired on disability from her job as a maintenance worker. Her annual household income totals $13,000 from disability and Work First. She has seven children and thirty-four grandchildren.

Dottie is financially responsible for her seven grandchildren as well as her 43-year-old daughter, who is unemployed and lives in the home. She takes care of her grandchildren because their mothers are abusing drugs and alcohol, and neglecting the children's needs. Although she is in very poor health, Dottie takes pride in raising her grandchildren. "They are my life, they make my day," she says. There are, however, some difficult spots. Getting them up for school is difficult because of Dottie's health problems. "I would like to go places without having to worry about my grandchildren. I need help with the children, and I need respite care," she says.

Grandmother Dottie reports that she has a wonderful and affectionate relationship with her grandchildren. However, their mothers are not involved in their lives. Their mothers do not call or visit very often. "The children love their mothers, but they don't seem to care if they come or go. They used to cry a lot, but now they are OK," says Dottie. Nor are the children's fathers involved in their lives. "Two of the children do not know their father," says Dottie.

Dottie's support network is sparse. She relies on her daughter who lives in the home, and God for her support. Because of her health problems, she does not attend church often. But, she says, "my spiritual beliefs uplift my spirits." Dottie has many values that have sustained her through difficult times. She values freedom, peace, privacy, comfort, good health, and being alone with no grandchildren to care for. Dottie's adopted parents taught her to help others, don't hold grudges, never turn children away, accept a child for what he is, and be the best that you can be. She thinks it's important to teach her grandchildren to be independent, responsible, stay together as a family, and be responsible for yourself. Dottie sees her role in the family as "someone everyone can count on, even my grown children. They always call me for help; they depend on me."

### Arlene—Age 53

**Household Composition**

| | |
|---|---|
| Daughter | 35 |
| Grandson | 16 |
| Grandson | 15 |
| Granddaughter | 12 |
| Granddaughter | 9 |

Arlene is a 53-year-old separated grandmother who is head of household for the home she owns in Orange County, North Carolina. She is a high-school graduate with two years of college. She is employed as a secretary, and has a household income of $35,000. In addition to her earnings, she receives financial assistance from Work First for her grandchildren. She has two children and four grandchildren.

Arlene has been taking care of her grandchildren for a total of twelve years. She assumed custodial care because of neglect and drug use by her daughter, the children's mother. She says that "raising grandchildren is special and I enjoy the time I spend with them." In spite of the joys, however, Arlene has a number of problems and concerns pertaining to the need for informal and formal support, and job conflicts. She does not get adequate support from her family, and would like for the children's mother to be more involved in their care. "I am frustrated and burned out, and need some relief from my child-care responsibilities," she says. She is concerned that she does not have sufficient time to take care of them, and the role of custodial caregiver conflicts with her job responsibilities. She describes her concerns regarding lack of government support,

Government will pay foster parents but not grandparents. This is a problem. In order to get financial support, you have to have foster parent status. Most grandparents don't go to Social Services because they fear that their funds will be taken away, or will be considered in any amount given to children if their incomes are reported. I don't feel that I have the kind of support I need.

The lack of financial support is exacerbated by poor relationships and lack of emotional support from her grandchildren's parents. The grandmother's relationship with her daughter, the children's mother, is strained, and she is concerned about her aberrant behavior and her relationship with her children.

I don't like what she does. I have no tolerance for her. She comes in and out of the home. She has been on drugs for ten years. The children resent their mother and they take it out on me. They hate what she is doing. I am concerned about how she will affect them later. The children rarely see their mother. The children love their mother and want to see her, but they do not want to live with her. The children's father lives with their mother, unmarried, but does not spend time with the children.

Arlene's family support is weak, but she relies on friends and God for much of her emotional support. She is a church member and attends church services and activities regularly. She says that her spiritual beliefs help her to know that "there is nothing I cannot do." Religion is among Arlene's many values. Others include life, family, mental and physical health, and hard work. Her parents taught her to love, share, respect others, and to love God. She thinks it's important to teach her grandchildren the importance of family, God, and success. Arlene says "everyone depends on me. Everyone looks to me to solve their problems. I am the strength."

### Louise—Age 55

#### Household Composition

| | |
|---|---|
| Father | 76 |
| Daughter | 35 |
| Grandson | 15 |
| Granddaughter | 12 |

Louise is a 55-year-old grandmother, who shares her home with her elderly father, her daughter, and two grandchildren. She is divorced, a high-school graduate, and has worked as a cook for most of her life. Her $30,000 household income is from her earnings, retirement benefits, and Work First for her grandchildren. She has one child and two grandchildren.

Louise takes care of her father, who has Alzheimer's Disease as well as her grandchildren. Her grandchildren are in her primary care because their mother neglected their needs and is abusing drugs and alcohol. She adds, "they have no place to live." When asked how she feels about being a grandparent caregiver at this time, she responds, "it's a lot of responsibility on me. I like to see them grow. But, sometimes, I feel that I don't have the freedom to do the things I want to do." Louise is clearly distressed and overwhelmed by the demands of custodial caregiving.

Like all of the grandparents in the study, Louise's concerns are centered around the needs of her grandchildren. She fears that they will get involved with drugs or get in serious trouble, or her granddaughter might get pregnant. "I hope I stay in good health, body and mind, to see them grow up," she says. The children's needs are primarily financial. They also need organized social activities and after-school programs.

Louise's relationship with her grandchildren is "good." But, she says,

Their relationship with their mother is poor. They love her, but my grandson does not respect her because of what she is doing. He does not respect her as a parent. She has not been a responsible mother and that affects my grandson deeply. My grandson wants to protect his mother, but my granddaughter does not show much emotion toward her mother.

The grandmother's relationship with the daughter is also strained. She gets no assistance from her daughter in caring for the children.

Although Louse receives little support from her daughter, who lives in the home, she is satisfied with the support she receives from other family members and friends. She attends church regularly and participates in church activities, but she receives no financial support from the church for the children. She does, however, receive emotional support and social support in the form of prayer, encouragement, visitation, and advice. She says, "just knowing there is a greater power gives me strength. When I'm worried or tense, I pray for relief."

Raised by her parents and an aunt, Louise was taught responsibility, respect, love, honesty, dependability, caring, understanding, and how to survive. She thinks it's important to teach her grandchildren honesty, dependability, and respect. She sees her role within the family as "the one who carries the load."

### Liz—Age 53

**Household Composition**

| | |
|---|---|
| Granddaughter | 13 |
| Grandson | 11 |
| Granddaughter | 8 |

Liz is a 53-year-old high-school graduate, who shares her mobile home with her three grandchildren. She is employed full-time as a clerical worker, and has an annual income of approximately $20,000 from earnings and a small amount from Work First. She has lived in her three-bedroom mobile home for twenty-three years. She has three children and five grandchildren.

Liz, clearly overwhelmed by responsibility, has been legal guardian for her three grandchildren for eight years. A combination of the parents' problems resulted in the grandmother assuming primary care; these include abuse of drugs and alcohol, neglect, incarceration or conviction of crimes at various times, emotional/mental problems, and teen pregnancy. Liz is skeptical about whether she can "survive the whole thing; I want them to grow up, so that I can enjoy life." She says that she likes custodial caregiving for her grandchildren, "but it takes a lot out of me. I should be enjoying life right now. I should be able to go and come as I please, but I can't. I don't have enough time to take care of them." Her situation is exacerbated by her financial troubles. She has to work full-time because she receives assistance for only one child.

Liz's caregiving responsibilities are related to a number of other problems. The children's father is awaiting trial for allegedly raping a white college student, and their mother is in prison on drug charges. The day I met with her, she was anxious about visiting her son in a nearby town some twenty miles away, although she had no transportation. She is overly concerned about the possible outcome of the trial, particularly because she does not have the money to afford an attorney. She is troubled that her son will have a criminal record. Her child-care burdens are made worse by her experiences with Social Services. She feels discouraged to apply for more assistance because of "their intrusion in my life, and still I might not get anything," she says. In spite of the burdens, however, Liz says that she feels good about being able to take care of her grandchildren. "I have no regrets. I wish things were different, but I don't mind taking care of them."

Liz's burdens are enormous, but her family and friends social support network is weak. She states that she would like to have more support from other relatives to help with the teenage years. "The teenage years are complicated because their attitudes change. This period is difficult for me. There are more negatives than positives in their lives, and I hope they can come out of it being responsible adults," she says.

Liz was raised by her mother and older sister who taught her responsibility, how to love, religion, importance of family, and to care for one another. She has maintained her childhood values, and has added health to that list. She thinks it's important to teach her grandchildren to be responsible adults, set good standards for themselves, develop good self-esteem, be their best, and do their best. She sees her role as "the backbone of the family."

## Loretta—Age 57

**Household Composition**

| | |
|---|---|
| Husband | 59 |
| Grandson | 13 |

Loretta is a 57-year-old gracious grandmother, who lives with her husband and grandson. She is a college graduate, who has worked for most of her adult life as a college recruitment specialist. She reports an annual household income of over $40,000. They live in their own home in an urban North Carolina town. Loretta has three children and one grandchild.

Loretta has raised her 13-year-old grandson since age 3, when her 35-year-old daughter decided that she could no longer care for him. When she began to neglect the child's needs, the grandparents made the decision to care for the child. Loretta reports that she has a wonderful relationship with her grandson and enjoys seeing him "grow and develop. My grandson keeps me younger, and more alert; he helps me keep up with the times." However, she is concerned about the relationship her grandson has with his mother. "She does not show any nurturing or mothering instincts toward the child," says Loretta. The grandchild has no contact with his father. She is concerned that her grandchild will feel that he has lost out on something because his parents were not around. The grandparents, however, are like parents to their grandchild, providing him with the unconditional love that he would normally receive from his parents.

Loretta is deeply religious and receives much social and emotional support from her family, friends, and church. She is a church member and involved in church activities several times per week. She says, "my spiritual beliefs keep me positive on a daily basis, enlightened, and I communicate better." Loretta was raised by her parents, and had a strong support network of extended family. She was taught love and respect. She values family, church, friendship, wholesome relationships, a well-rounded life, and togetherness. She thinks it's important to teach her grandchild to understand what it means to love God, and what it takes to sustain himself. Grandmother Loretta sees her role as "the glue that holds the family together."

### Lydia—Age 53

**Household Composition**

| Granddaughter | 8 |
| Granddaughter | 5 |

Lydia is a 53-year-old divorced grandmother who is primary caregiver for her two granddaughters in Orange County, North Carolina. She is a high-school graduate and a retired teacher's aid. Her annual income from a retirement pension and family support is $12,000. Lydia lives in a mobile home that she owns. She does not receive any financial assistance from Social Services.

Lydia feels good that she is able to provide a stable environment for her grandchildren. Besides her custodial care responsibilities, Lydia takes care of four other grandchildren on a part-time basis. She has been primary caregiver for three years, and hopes that her daughter will return to reclaim her children soon. She is among the many grandmothers in the study who do not want to take care of their grandchildren. She feels that it's her obligation. "I feel forced into taking on these responsibilities," she says. Many grandmothers resent this intrusion, particularly at a time when they are just beginning to enjoy their retirement or after they have completed raising their own children.

Lydia assumed custodial care for her grandchildren after learning that her daughter was on drugs, left the children at a friend's house, and did not return to retrieve them. Lydia was contacted by Social Services who requested her help. Presently, she has only temporary custody. She says, "there needs to be a law requiring mothers and fathers to take care of their own children instead of putting them off on grandparents." She is very adamant about not wanting to take care of her grandchildren. She says, "I am angry and frustrated because I am stuck with the day-to-day responsibility of taking care of them. Their mother has her life, but I have none." Lydia is outraged that the parents do not have any responsibility to care for their own children. I asked why she chose to accept the responsibility and she replied,

They are my blood. I had to take them because I did not know what would happen to them if they were in foster care. Would they get good care? I had to take them, although I did not want them. This is a hard thing to do. The most difficult aspect of child care is having to break my routine. When I retired, I wanted to enjoy myself. Having to start all over with discipline gets on my nerves. I don't like having to start all over again. I have no social life. Just a basic thing like going to the bank, is a problem. I am restricted in my normal activities. My life has changed. It's harder raising grandchildren than your own. Things have changed. Everything is more expensive. Raising my own children was simpler.

Lydia's attitude about taking care of her grandchildren, although extreme, is not uncommon in it's overall demeanor. Many of today's grandmothers are younger than the traditional age for grandparents, and are not prepared socially, emotionally, or financially for the new role responsibilities. Lydia's attitude is clearly among the strongest for disliking her caregiving role. She is concerned about whether she will be able to get through this. She asks, "Will I have them for the rest of my life?" In spite of the pain and entrapment she feels, she seems to be consoled by the notion that they have a safe place to live, and are being taken care of well.

Lydia relies on her family for social support and God for emotional support. She says that God plays a big role in helping her care for her grandchildren. "Prayer gets me through the day," she says. Along with her religious values, Lydia has maintained other traditional values that have contributed to her character. These include love of family, health, life, peace of mind, and motivation. Lydia's parents taught her to love; honor her mother and father; the importance of self-worth, education, kindness, and respect for the elderly. Lydia describes her role within the family as "role model" and "setter of family values."

### Beth—Age 51

**Household Composition**

| | |
|---|---|
| Grandson | 10 |
| Granddaughter | 7 |

Beth is a 51-year-old high-school graduate who is primary caregiver for two of her grandchildren. She has a full-time job as Human Resources Case Manager, and earns nearly $30,000 annually. Her income is supplemented by Work First and her ex-husband. In addition to owning her own home, she has other real estate property. Beth grew up in an extended family in rural North Carolina with four brothers and four sisters. She worked in the cotton fields as did most Southern blacks at the time. She spoke sadly about her four siblings who died of cancer in their early fifties; believing that eating clay dirt as youngsters contributed to the death of her two brothers.

Beth assumed care of her grandchildren soon after their birth. She is now legal guardian for both grandchildren. The grandmother is not clear about why she is caring for her grandchildren. She only says that "their mother is not responsible. I want them to be safe. I want them to have the same opportunities as their mother had—a good, safe, and clean environment." The mother's pattern of neglecting the children's needs and lack of attachment, described by the grandmother, is consistent with drug use. The grandchildren's relationship with their mother is strained. Said Beth, "My daughter has not bonded with her children, she does not call them, does not speak to them about life or school issues, and does not seem to be generally interested in them." The 10-year-old has not seen his father in seven years, and the 7-year-old has never seen her father. The grandmother is in distress over why her daughter would treat her own children this way, she says, "I've given her everything." Beth says the most difficult aspects of custodial care is that her relationships have suffered. "People who are not raising grandchildren, or don't have grandchildren, don't want to be bothered with my grandchildren," she says.

Beth has a number of concerns regarding her grandchildren and their mother's lack of involvement in their lives,

I worry that my grandchildren may not develop a positive self-esteem, because they are not with their parents. In addition to more financial support, a major concern for me as a grandmother caregiver is that I may not be able to let go of them when it's time for them to make their own choices. I have a mothering need, and I have problems letting go when I should. Maybe I need a counselor. I am resentful that my daughter will not take care of her own children. I feel that she is taking advantage of me. In some ways, I feel responsible for my daughter's behavior, because my ex-husband and I gave her everything, and we continue to do so even though she is 29 years old.

However, in spite of the problems, Beth says that she needs her grandchildren and enjoys taking care of them. "They are a blessing as well as a burden. I enjoy being there for them. They make me feel like I can do anything. I feel good about myself. I like the idea of getting parenting right this time."

Like the majority of grandparents in the study, Beth has a weak social support network and relies on God when she needs someone to help her. She says, "we pray a lot because prayer helps me with the punishment. I use the scriptures instead of punishment. Faith gives me patience, and helps me to be a better person."

Beth has some traditional African American values, such as religion, love of family, compassion, work ethic, acceptance of others, education, and inner peace. She was raised by her mother and grandmother, who taught her about the importance of education, to be respectful, to work for what you want, not to take things that you don't work for, to make sacrifices, to take care of home first, and to maintain proper behavior because what you do represents the family. Beth teaches her grandchildren to love one another, have good moral values, give back to the community, be productive citizens, love God, be happy, live a full life, and show respect to others. Beth describes herself as the "guardian."

## EMERGING THEMES AND DISCUSSION

A number of dominant themes emerged from the research. Among these were family structure, assumption of the caregiver role, common problems, unusual circumstances of caregiving, coping with the caregiving, self-perceptions of the caregiver role, and family values.

### Family Structure

The five most prominent family structural patterns that emerged from the study are as follows:

- Grandmother/grandchildren/great-grandchildren/nieces and nephews
- Grandmother/adult child/grandchildren
- Grandmother/grandfather/grandchildren
- Grandmother/grandchildren/fictive kin
- Grandmother/minor children/grandchildren

#### Grandmother/grandchildren/great-grandchildren/nieces and nephews

This was the most common pattern reported. Relationships and family interactions revolved around the needs of the grandchildren and other minors in the household. Family interactions in this type of structure were more effective than in any of the other four patterns. Effectiveness of family interactions were based on the amount of conflict among family members. Grandmother-only households with grandchildren were more organized and less conflict-oriented.

### Grandmother/adult child/grandchildren

This pattern was more conflict-oriented. Disagreements were centered primarily around child-rearing issues between the grandmother and her daughter. Most often, an adult child living in the household may not relieve the grandmother of child-care duties. Since the vast majority of grandmothers were caring for grandchildren because of the drug use of their children, the conflict was often related to the lack of attention given to children by their mothers. Most grandmothers did not want their daughters in the household.

### Grandmother/grandfather/grandchildren

This pattern consisted of grandmothers caring for their grandchildren and ailing husbands. Even in cases where husbands were not sick, only a small number assisted with the child-care duties. Spousal relationships consisted of many older women trying desperately to hold their marriages together after many years of abuse by their husbands. The majority of the 26 percent of married women in the sample had endured many years of psychological and physical abuse from their husbands. This suggests the need for family intervention and mental health services for these custodial grandmothers as well as their spouses.

### Grandmother/grandchild/fictive kin

This pattern was less conflict-oriented than either of the two previous types. "Fictive kin" is a concept developed by Carol Stack (1974), and refers to nonrelated individuals who have taken on family roles, but who are not related by blood. Fictive kin in grandmother-headed households consisted primarily of male companions. Their roles consisted of providing financial assistance, as well as emotional support for the entire family. Most often these were males whose incomes were not sufficient enough to maintain independent households.

### Grandmother/minor children/grandchildren

Most of the young grandmothers had minor children of their own living in the home. In such cases, the grandmother assumed total care of the grandchildren and raised them as their own. Relationships with the grand-child and their mother were often more like that of siblings, rather than mother and child.

In all family structures, the most effective relationships were between grandchildren and grandparents; and the least effective ones were between the grandchildren and their parents. The following patterns are characteristics of family relationships.

- Grandmother–grandchild: frequent contact and loving relationships.
- Grandchild–biological mother: sporadic contact, most often relationships are not loving; little contact; little involvement in the child's daily activities.
- Grandmother–daughter: strained interactions.
- Grandchild–biological father: no meaningful contact; the child rarely if ever sees the father.
- Mother–father: no meaningful contact.

Grandmother–grandchild relationships were often described as loving and caring. Mother–child relationships often fragmented and inconsistent. Grandmother–daughter relationships were strained at best and ineffective. Father–child relationships were almost always nonexistent. Many were incarcerated, and those who were not in jail, took little interest in their children as reported by grandmothers. Many of the grandchildren in the study did not know their biological father. Some 80 percent of the grandmothers reported that the child's mother had little or no contact with the child's biological father.

### Assumption of the Caregiver Role

Custodial caregiving among the African American grandmothers in this study was a burden as well as a blessing. The majority of them (approximately 60 percent) had mixed feelings about caring for their grandchildren. Some of their concerns were lack of financial support, their own failing health, the need for respite care, the permanence of child-care responsibilities, and inadequate housing. Another 20 percent reported having no problems and truly enjoyed caring for their grandchildren. Their grandchildren provided support and companionship. Approximately 20 percent reported not enjoying being a grandparent caregiver and not wanting to care for their grandchildren; they felt trapped in the position and very angry about their grandchildren being thrust onto them either by Social Services or their own children.

Grandmothers who had mixed feelings were often those with little informal support, financial worries, or children with health problems. The grandmothers in this category were, at first, not psychologically prepared to accept the burden of childcare but gradually assumed the role.

Approximately 20 percent of the grandmothers in the study did not want to take care of their grandchildren and were resentful of the children's parents. A majority of the grandmothers in the study did want to take care of their grandchildren under these adverse conditions. It not only involves full-time caregiving, but also a permanent commitment to long-term care. Their emotional and social problems are aggravated by the need for financial support, respite care, after-school care, and summer programs.

### Problems

Grandmothers experienced a broad range of problems. Many of these are listed here, but not in order of priority.

- School system
- Coresident adult child
- Lack of formal support (financial)
- Lack of informal support (social and emotional)
- Poor housing
- Respite care
- Health problems of grandchildren
- Health problems of grandparent
- Competing family demands
- Abrupt assumption of the caregiver role
- Impact of AIDS
- Impact of incarcerations
- Impact of crack cocaine
- Poor family relationships
- Long-term commitment
- Educational needs of grandparent and grandchildren
- Special needs of teenage grandchildren

### Unusual Circumstances of Caregiving

Unusual circumstances were described as situations where grandmothers must care for grandchildren in circumstances involving, not only grandchildren, but under conditions which result in grandparenting being much more challenging and demanding.

Here are four of the most serious situations:

- Grandmother caring for nine grandchildren all under 14 years old.
- Legally blind grandmother with eight grandchildren.
- Grandmother with four grandsons, all sick and under 12 years old.
- Grandmother with four grandchildren under 5 years old living in substandard housing.

In spite of the demands placed on grandparents, however, the majority enjoyed taking care of their grandchildren.

## Coping with Caregiving: The Role of Religion

Ninety-two percent of the grandmothers in the sample reported being a member of a religious institution. Eight percent reported no church affiliation. Almost all grandmothers reported a strong reliance on God and prayer to help them cope with the problems and issues of caregiving and to help get them through the day. Religion was reported as the most important value. Most reported relying on God for their emotional support instead of a friend or relative. Regarding coping and the role of religion, the general consensus was that grandmothers felt if they had God in their lives, they did not need anyone else. This is a reflection of their strong spiritual foundation, and the meaning of religion the African American women in this study incorporate into their daily lives.

## Self-Perceptions of Grandmother Functions in the Caregiver Role

We wanted to know how grandmothers viewed themselves based on their role as grandparent caregiver. A wide range of responses were provided as indicated here.

| Grandmothers' Self-Perceptions | N (total number) |
| --- | --- |
| Mother/guardian/matriarch/nurturer/caretaker | 20 |
| Supporter/provider | 19 |
| Strength/pillar/glue/backbone | 16 |
| Many different things (doctor/problem-solver/ enabler/peacemaker/banker/counselor/doctor) | 15 |
| Advisor | 10 |
| Spiritual leader/teacher/source of wisdom | 10 |
| Maid | 9 |
| Role model | 5 |
| Friend | 3 |

## Family Values

Vital to the existence of the intergenerational family is a mutual support system centered around economic subsistence. Intergenerational families also provide emotional and social support. Those in need, usually adult children, often turn to the grandmother-maintained family unit for help. The mutual support within the extended family is the glue that holds the unit together. Without the ongoing exchange of goods and services, many of the family members would not be able to survive.

The fundamental values that have sustained African American families are well documented in the literature (Billingsley 1992; Gary et al. 1983; Hill 1971; Stack 1974). Billingsley (1992) identified a set of values contributing to stability and achievement. Among these were spirituality, educational achievement, strong family ties, and economic independence. Another set of values identified by Gary and associates (1983) included strong kinship ties, strong achievement orientation, strong religious orientation, positive parent–child relationships, and strong work orientation. The most ground-breaking research in the area was conducted by Robert Hill and published in his book *The Strengths of Black Families* (1971). Hill identified such values as strong kinship bonds, strong work orientation, adaptability of family roles, strong achievement orientation, and strong religious orientation. Stack (1974) in her study of black families found strong emphasis on relationships, kinship ties, reciprocity, and strong commitment to children.

In this study of grandmother-maintained households, we found a similar set of values. We asked grandmothers about their values in three different categories: values they were taught by their parents, values they presently hold, and values they are teaching their grandchildren. Values taught while growing up included strong religious orientation, family ties, education, respect for elders, respect for authority, self-reliance, honesty, hard work, educational achievement, and helping others. Values they presently hold include religious orientation, strong family ties, love and strong commitment to children, health, education, hard work, safety, financial security, helping others, self-development, inner peace, and self-reliance. Findings showed that values they were taught varied somewhat from those they presently hold. Namely safety, health, and self-development (e.g., self-discipline, goal-setting, motivation, and self-esteem). Respect for elders sharply declined, whereas emphasis on wealth accumulation increased. These values are directly related to the problems and issues of contemporary living, and were not as serious fifty or sixty years ago when they were growing up. Finally, the values they are teaching their grandchildren include religious orientation, education, strong family ties, respect for elders, helping others, good morals, honesty, and self-development. There is much stronger emphasis on self-development issues in this category. Among those reported are discipline, determination, motivation, happiness, dependability, responsibility, kindness, independence, cleanliness, self-confidence, self-esteem, self-respect, and productivity.

The results from the value orientation aspect of the study emphasized the importance of traditional values such as religion, family, love of children, work, and education. However, it's important to note that as societies change, so do values. The variation from traditional values held by grandmothers in the sample represent the increasing complexity of the American society.

# Conclusion: Summary
# and Implications

The primary objective of this research was to make a contribution to the existing literature on the experiences as well as the sociodemographic, psychological, and physical health characteristics of custodial African American grandmothers. There is a greater prevalence of grandmother-headed households in African American families (Szinovacz 1998). We found that 74 percent were unmarried and heads of household. The grandmothers ranged in age from 38 to 88 with a mean age of 58. The average family income was $21,100. Thirty-three percent had incomes below $10,000. The number-one reason for providing care, consistent with existing literature and census reports, was abuse of drugs and alcohol by the parents of the grandchildren. The grandmothers in the sample had a number of chronic physical health conditions that often interfered with child-care responsibilities. Conditions such as arthritis, problems breathing, circulation problems, and kidney problems all interfered with activities of daily living. More than 15 percent of the grandmothers reported having seven of the ten chronic conditions listed in the study. In spite of the observed stress, only 19 percent of the grandmothers scored in the range for depressive symptomatology as measured by a modified CES-D Scale. It is very likely that a stress or anxiety measure could be more appropriate.

The grandparenting role presents a number of problems for grand-mother caregivers. Problems include not having enough money to get the things they needed, not having enough time for themselves, not being able to attend church, lost friendships, the need for after-school and summer programs, poor health, inability to discipline properly, inability to negoti-ate school problems, lack of cooperation and support from parents, lack of parental involvement in the child's life, and social abuse from the grand-parents' children.

In cases where grandparents are elderly, this problem along with many others become much more serious for the grandchild as well as the grand-parent caregiver. Twenty-six percent of the grandparents in our study were 65 and older. Grandmothers love their children and feel that they are pro-viding the best care, however, more research is needed to determine the quality of care concerning different issues of caregiving. Although grand-parent care seems to be the next best thing to parents, more attention needs to be given to the impact of grandparent caregiving on grandchil-dren with respect to parenting skills on the grandchild's development. The vast majority of the children were born to single mothers. Most children did not know their father or had little or no contact with him, and most had little or no relationship with their mother. In cases where there was a relationship with the mother, it was often inconsistent and strained. More research is needed to address the complex social interactions between grandchildren and parents, and how they might affect the long-term suc-cess of children who are in the care of grandparents.

All but a few grandmothers in this sample stated that they felt over-whelmed by the responsibility. Burton (1992) found that grandparents fre-quently requested respite care for parenting. However, out of guilt that they might have failed as parents, and out of fear that child protective services might remove the children from their care, African American grandmothers are often reluctant to seek opportunities for a break. In comparison to younger grandmothers, older African American grandmothers report feel-ing less overwhelmed by responsibility, and their attitudes about caregiving were generally more approving. Older African American women place care-giving at the forefront of their existence. Caregiving helps older African American women define who they are and their worth in society. The sacri-fices they make for their children and grandchildren are central to their belief system concerning their roles as women and their devotion to chil-dren, which is shaped by their West African heritage. Older women's beliefs about family, and the extended family network, have a strong influ-ence on their attitudes about caregiving roles. Although the support of the extended family has a long history in black American culture, it can no longer shield grandmothers from the burdens and stresses of caregiving brought on by the crack-cocaine epidemic, AIDS, and the incarceration of young African American mothers. Once the norm in African American families, changes in family structure and the impact of societal problems have contributed to the erosion of extended family support.

The head-of-household status of the grandmother increases her role responsibilities within the family unit. She is not only the "guardian of the

generations" as described by E. Franklin Frazier (1939), she describes herself in the present study as caretaker, nurturer, role model, setter of family
values, maid, spiritual teacher, advisor, leader, source of wisdom, one who
keeps the family together, financial provider, social and emotional supporter, mother, father, and everything to everyone. In spite of her age,
frailty, or financial status, the custodial African American grandmother is
typically depended upon by all members within the family unit, as well as
grown children not living in the home. African American grandmothers not
only provide social, emotional, and financial support to their children, they
also server as enablers for them which encourages dependency. For example, one frail 78-year-old grandmother does the laundry for a grown
healthy daughter using wash tubs. Aware that her mother did not have
laundry facilities, the daughter did not seem to be concerned about how the
job got done. Another elderly grandmother cared for three teenage boys,
while her son lived in the home providing no financial support and no
child-care assistance. Grandparents were routinely taken advantage of by
their grown children. However, in spite of the overwhelming responsibility,
African American grandmothers take pride in their role as caregivers.

Researchers must focus on the needs of unmarried custodial grandmothers. There is little empirical research on the impact of raising grandchildren
on African American grandmothers. In spite of the increasing numbers of
grandparent caregivers in the population, not much is known about the
broad social and demographic characteristics of African American grandmothers. Longitudinal studies are needed to get a closer look at the long-
term effects of caregiving on African American grandmothers.

The circumstances under which grandparents assume care of their
grandchildren have not been well researched. We believe that research on
this issue would broaden our understanding of the transition from parental
care to grandparent care. In addition to the process of how children came
to the care of grandparents, more information is needed concerning how
informed African American grandmothers are in providing care at different stages of the grandchild's social and emotional development. Although
many similarities exist among African American and white custodial
grandmother caregivers, many differences are present (Fuller-Thomson,
Minkler, and Driver 1998; Szinovacz 1998). The meaning of caregiving
across different racial and ethnic groups, suggests different needs for
research and program development.

The lack of informal support was common among these grandmothers.
Although some studies have suggested that the traditional extended family
network in African American communities is an important source of social
support (Billingsley 1992; Hill 1997; Martin and Martin 1985), grandmother caregivers in this study received little support from family and
friends. Grandmothers relied heavily on their faith, and often cited God as
their only source of support. Only two of the ninety-nine grandmothers in

the sample reported receiving help in some form from the African American church. George, Blazer, and Hughes (1989) found that high levels of social support are associated with decreased levels of psychiatric morbidity, particularly depression.

This study is particularly meaningful in that African American grandmothers are as diverse in their socioeconomic characteristics as they are in attitudes about caregiving and their styles of delivering care. While some enjoy the challenge, many feel trapped and obligated, and others clearly resent the role. More research and programs need to address the resentment that these African American grandmothers feel as a result of being primary caregivers. The traditional meaning of the social support network has clearly broken down in these communities. The high volume of support that black families once received is no longer available to all grandmothers.

There is a need for support services for grandmothers, particularly respite care. Under the Older American's Act, states can use National Family Caregiver Support Program (NFCSP) funds to provide services such as respite care for grandmother caregivers (65 and older) of children under 18 years of age. In addition, perhaps policy makers should consider extending NFCSP eligibility to younger grandmothers, or providing funds for a similar program for them. Younger grandmothers are experiencing more depression and it's probably because of multiple demands on their time since many are still working. Respite care, a primary service offered through NFCSP, may be more important to their well-being than to older grandmothers. Policy makers and practitioners must develop policies and programs that assist grandparent caregivers in continuing to provide for their grandchildren by building strong family units and coping with the demands of caregiving that can adversely affect their physical and psychological well-being.

Several limitations must be taken into account concerning this sample of custodial grandmother caregivers. This sample included only grandmothers who were mobile, and generally healthy, with only a few debilitating problems. We do not know what differences there might be among custodial caregivers who are less mobile, and who have more severe health conditions. The sample does not represent a broad range of income, education, and occupational differences. However, in spite of these limitations, there are specific characteristics in this sample which have similarities to national data (Bryson and Casper 1999; Fuller-Thomson, Minkler, and Driver 1998; Szinovacz 1998). We hope this volume has given a more distinct picture of the characteristics and plight of African American grandmothers who are primary caregivers in intergenerational households. Perhaps we can refocus our attention on the need to support families maintained by grandmothers by assisting them in developing strong family units. Policies that support intergenerational families must be an ongoing agenda in the twenty-first century.

In conclusion, the role of African American grandmothers has not changed as much as their level of involvement in care responsibilities for their grandchildren. Specifically, this study reaffirms the discoveries of prior studies that the circumstances under which grandmothers provide care have changed.

Two patterns of caregiver role assumption emerged from open-ended qualitative results: *immediate assumption* and *gradual assumption*. Immediate assumption, which was observed in about 75% of the sample, was reflected in reports of grandmothers who were thrust suddenly into the custodial caregiving role without previous warning. Examples of immediate caregiving role assumption included the biological parent (typically the mother) leaving the child in the grandmother's care and failing to return, intervention by Social Services because the mother neglected the child's needs, discovery by the grandmother that the child was unattended for an unreasonable period of time, and incarceration of the parent. *Gradual assumption,* which was observed in about 25% of the sample, referred to grandmothers who had previous, and sometimes regular, experience caring for grandchildren. Examples included caring for grandchildren when at least one biological parent was living in the grandparents' home sporadically, or caring for grandchildren while a parent was receiving drug or alcohol treatment. These seemingly temporary situations could become permanent once a parent moved out and left children with grandparents, or if the parent was unable to maintain sobriety.

Custodial caregiving among African American grandmothers was observed to be a burden as well as a blessing. While a majority of the grandmothers in this study (approximately 60%) reported they enjoyed caring for their grandchildren, grandmothers were nonetheless concerned about inadequate financial support, poor health, the need for respite care, being saddled with permanent childcare responsibilities, and inadequate housing. Twenty percent of grandmothers had mixed feelings about having responsibility for their grandchildren's care. Another 20% did not enjoy being a grandparent caregiver, felt trapped in the position, and felt angry about grandchildren's care being thrust onto them by either the children's parents or by Social Services.

In spite of their mixed feelings, grandmothers in the study generally assumed care and remained in the role of caregiving for a number of reasons including (1) a deeply felt sense of obligation to their grandchildren, (2) the need to keep their grandchildren out of the system, (3) the need to control the "proper" upbringing of the child, and (4) the need to care for others. Further, many grandmothers felt that raising their grandchildren was special, and they enjoyed the time spent with them. Many took pride in continuing their traditional roles as guardian, caregiver, and conveyers of African American family values and felt blessed in many ways to have their grandchildren live with them. Mary, an 88 year-old grandmother, says, "There is nothing difficult about raising children. When you love children, nothing is hard. I have raised 45 children and that is what I do best."

Alleviating the caregiving burden of custodial grandparents will require not only support for them and their grandchildren but also efforts to ameliorate social problems.

# References

Adams, D. L. 1969. Analysis of a life satisfaction index. *Journal of Gerontology* 24:470–474.

Aneshensel, C., R. Frerichs, and G. Huba. 1984. Depression and physical illness: A multiwave, nonrecursive model. *Journal of Health and Social Behavior* 25:350–371.

Aschenbrenner, 1973. Extended families among black Americans. *Journal of Comparative Family Studies* 4:257–268.

Barnhill, S. 1996. Three generations at risk: The imprisoned women, their children, and the grandmother caregiver. *Generations,* 20(1): 39(2).

Beckman, E., and W. Leber. 1995. *Handbook of depression.* 2nd. ed. New York: New York Press.

Best, Felton. 1998. *Black religious leadership from the slave community to the million man march.* New York: The Edwin Mellen Press.

Billingsley, A. 1992. *Climbing Jacob's ladder: The enduring legacy of African American families.* New York: Simon and Schuster.

Blassingame, J. W. 1972. *The slave community: Plantation life in the antebellum South.* New York: Oxford University Press.

Blazer, D., B. Burchett, C. Service, and L. George. 1991. The association of age and depression among the elderly: An epidemiologic exploration. *Journal of Gerontology* 46(6): M210–215.

Brown, D. R., and D. B. Monye. 1995. *Midlife and older African Americans as intergenerational caregivers of school-aged children.* AARP Andrus Foundation Final Report.

Bryson, K. and L. Casper. 1999. Co-resident grandparents and grandchildren. U.S. Census Bureau, Current Population Reports, Special Studies, 23–198, Washington, DC.

Burnette, D. 1999. Physical and emotional well-being of custodial grandparents in Latino families. *American Journal of Orthopsychiatry* 69(3): 305–318.

Burton, L. M. 1992. Black grandparents rearing children of drug-addicted parents: Stressors, outcomes and social service needs. *The Gerontologist* 32(6): 744–751.

Burton, L. M., and C. DeVries. 1993. Challenges and rewards: African American grandparents as surrogate parents. In *Families and aging,* ed. L. M. Burton. Amityville, NY: Baywood.

Casper, L. M., and K. R. Bryson. 1998. *Coresident grandparents and their grandchildren: Grandparent-maintained families.* U.S. Bureau of the Census, Population Division, Fertility and Family Statistics Branch.

Close, Stacy. 1998. Sending up some timber: Elderly slaves and religious leadership in the antebellum slave community. *Black religious leadership from the slave community to the million-man march,* ed. Felton Best. New York: The Edwin Mellen Press.

Creel, Margaret Washington. 1988. *The particular people: Slave religion and community culture among the Gullahs.* Chicago: Chicago University Press.

Davidhizar, R., G. A. Bechtel, and B. C. Woodring. 2000. The changing role of grandparenthood. *Journal of Gerontological Nursing* 26:24–29.

Davis, E. 1992. *Grandparents as parents: Raising a second generation.* Special Congressional Committee on Aging. Serial No. 102-24.

Dressel, P., and S. Barnhill. 1994. Reframing gerontological thought and practice: The case of grandmothers with daughters in prison. *The Gerontologist* 34:685–690.

Du Bois, W. E. B. 1920, 1975. *Darkwater: Voices from within the veil.* New York: Schocken Books.

Du Bois, W. E. B. 1962. *Black reconstruction in America: 1860–1888.* New York: Simon and Schuster.

Emick, M., and B. Hayslip Jr. 1996. Custodial grandparenting: New roles for middle-aged and older adults. *International Journal of Aging and Human Development* 43(2): 135–154.

Forsyth, C. J., S. B. Roberts, and C. A. Robin. 1992. Variables influencing life satisfaction among grandparents. *International Journal of Sociology of the Family* 22:51–60.

Frazier, E. F. 1939. *The Negro family in the United States.* Chicago: University of Chicago Press.

Frazier, E. F. 1957. *The Negro in the United States.* Toronto: Macmillan.

Fuller-Thomson, E., M. Minkler, and D. Driver. 1997. A profile of grandparents raising granchildren in the United States. *Gerontologist* 37:406–411.

Gary, L. E., L. A. Beatty, G. Berry, and M. D. Price. 1983. *Stable Black Families: Final Report.* Washington, DC: Institute for Urban Affairs and Research.

Genovese, E. D. 1976. *Roll, Jordan, roll: The world the slaves made.* New York: Vintage Books.

George, L. 1995. Social factors and illness. In *Handbook of Aging and the Social Sciences,* 4th ed., eds. R. H. Binstock and L. K. George, 229–252. New York: Academic Press.

George, L. K. 1992. Social factors and the onset and outcome of depression. In *Aging, health behaviors, and health outcomes,* eds. K. W. Schaie, J. S. House, and D. G. Blazer, 137–159. Hillsdale, NJ: Lawrence Erlbaum Associates.

George, L. K., D. G. Blazer, D. C. Hughes, and N. Fowler. 1989. Social support and the outcome of major depression. *British Journal of Psychiatry* 154:478–485.

Gilkes, Cheryl T. 1993. Religion. In *Black women in America: An historical encyclopedia,* ed. Darlene Clark Hine. Brooklyn, NY: Carlson Publishing.

Guthrie, P. 1995. Mother Mary Ann Wright: African-American women, spirituality, and social activism. In *Women's spirituality, women's lives,* eds. J. Ochshorn and E. Cole, 165. New York: Haworth Press.

Gutman, D. 1976. *Black family in slavery and freedom (1950–1952).* New York: Pantheon Books.

Haley, W. E., C. A. C. West, V. G. Wadley, G. R. Ford, F. A. White, J. J. Barrett, L. E. Harrell, and D. L. Roth. 1995. Psychological, social, and health impact of caregiving: A comparison of black and white dementia family caregivers and noncaregivers. *Psychology and Aging* 10:540–552.

Hayes, Diana. 1995. *Hagar's daughters: Womanist ways of being in the world.* New York: Paulist Press.

Hayslip, B., R. Shore, C. Henderson, and P. Lambert. 1998. Custodial grandparenting and the impact of grandchildren with problems on role satisfaction and role meaning. *Journal of Gerontology: Social Sciences* 53B(3): S164–S173.

Hill, R. 1971. *The strengths of black families.* New York: Emerson-Hall.

Hill, R. 1997. The strengths of the African-American family: Twenty-five years later. Washington, DC: Rand Publishing.

Hill-Lubin, M. 1991. The African American grandmother in autobiographical works by Frederick Douglass, Langston Hughes, and Maya Angelou. *Journal of Aging and Human Development* 33:173–185.

Honey, E. 1998. AIDS and the inner city: Critical issues. *Social Casework: The Journal of Contemporary Social Work* June: 365–370.

hooks, b. 1981. *Ain't I a woman?* Boston: Pluto Press.

Hoyt, Danny R., and James C. Creech. 1983. The Life Satisfaction Index: A methodological and theoretical critique. *Journal of Gerontology* 38:111–116.

Jones, J. 1985. *Labor of love, labor of sorrow.* New York: Vintage Books.

Kee, D. M. 1997. *Grandparents as caregivers of adolescent granchildren.* M.A. Thesis. California State University, Long Beach.

Kelley, S. J. 1993. Caregiver stress in grandparents raising grandchildren. *Journal of Nursing Scholarship* 25(4): 331–337.

Ladner, J. 1971. *Tomorrow's tomorrow.* New York: Anchor Books.

Ladner, J. and Gourdine, R. 1984. Intergenerational teenage motherhood: Some preliminary findings. *A Scholarly Journal of Black Women* 1(2): 22–24.

LeBlanc, A., A. London, and C. Aneshensel. 1997. The physical costs of AIDS caregiving. *Social Science and Medicine* 45(6): 915–923.

Liang, Jersey. 1984. "Dimensions of the Life Satisfaction Index A: A structural formulation." *Journal of Gerontology* 39:613–622.

Lohr, M. J., M. J. Essex, and M. H. Klein. 1988. The relationships of coping responses to physical health status and life satisfaction among older women. *Journal of Gerontology* 43:54–60.

Martin, E. P., and J. M. Martin. 1985. *The helping tradition in the Black family and the community*. Silver Spring, MD: NASW.

Minkler, M., and E. Fuller-Thomson. 1999. The health of grandparents raising grandchildren: Results of a national study. *American Journal of Public Health* 89:1384–1389.

Minkler, M., E. Fuller-Thomson, D. Miller, and D. Driver. 1997. Depression in grandparents raising grandchildren: Results of a national longitudinal study. *Archives of Family Medicine* 6:445–452.

Minkler, M., and K. Roe. 1993. *Grandmothers as caregivers. Raising children of the crack-cocaine epidemic*. Newbury Park, CA: Sage.

Minkler, M., and K. Roe. 1996. Grandparents as surrogate parents. *Generation* 20:34–38.

Minkler, M., K. M. Roe, and M. Price. 1992. The physical and emotional health of grandmothers raising grandchildren in the crack-cocaine epidemic. *Gerontologist* 32:752–761.

Minkler, M., K. Roe, and R. Robertson-Beckley. 1994. Raising grandchildren from crack-cocaine households: Effects on family and friendship ties of African-American women. *American Journal of Orthropsychiatry* 64:20–29.

Musil, C. 1998. Health, stress, coping, and social support in grandmother caregivers. *Health Care for Women International* 19:441–455.

Neighbors, H. W. 1986. "Socioeconomic status and psychological distress in adult Blacks." *American Journal of Epidemiology* 124:779–792.

Neugarten, B. L., R. J. Havighurst, and S. S. Tobin. 1961. The measurement of life satisfaction. *Journal of Gerontology* 16:134–143.

Poe, L. 1992. Black grandparents as parents. Library of Congress: 616-580.

Pollard, L. 1981. Aging and slavery: A gerontological perspective. *Journal of Negro History* 66(3): 228–234.

Powdermaker, H. 1969. *After freedom: A cultural study in the Deep South*. New York: Antheneum.

Pruchno, R. 1999. Raising grandchildren: The experiences of black and white grandmothers. *The Gerontologist* 39(2): 209–221.

Quarles, B. 1964. *The Negro in the Making of America*. London: Collier-Macmillan.

Radloff, L. S. 1977. CES-D Scale: A self-report depression scale for research in a general population. *Applied Psychological Measurement* 3:385–401.

Raymond, E., and T. Michaels. 1980. Prevalence of correlates of depression in elderly persons. *Psychological Reports* 47:1055–1061.

Roe, K., M. Minkler, and R. Barnwell. 1994. The assumption of caregiving: Grandmothers raising the children of the crack-cocaine epidemic. *Qualitative Health Research* 4(3): 281–303.

Ruiz, D. 2000. Guardian and caretakers: African American grandmothers as primary caregivers in intergenerational families. *African American Research Perspectives* 6(1): 1–12.

Ruiz, D. and I. Carlton-LaNey. 1999. The increase in intergenerational African families headed by grandmothers. *Journal of Sociology and Social Welfare* 26(4): 71–86.

Ruiz, D. S., C. W. Zhu, and M. R. Crowther. 2003. *Not* on their own again: Psychological, social, and health characteristics of custodial American grandmothers. In *Widows and Divorce in Later Life: On Their Own Again*, ed. C. Jenkins. NewYork: Haworth.

Ruiz, D. S., C. W. Zhu, and M. R. Crowther. 2004. Social, demographic, and health characteristics of custodial African American grandmothers. In *Victimizing Vulnerable Groups: Images of Uniquely High Risk Crime Targets*, ed. C. Coston. Westport, CT: Praeger.

Sands, R. G. and R. S. Goldberg-Glen. 1996. The impact of surrogate parenting on grandparents: Stress, well-being, and life satisfaction. Andrus Foundation of the American Association of Retired Persons (AARP) Final Report. Research Information Center, 601 E. Street NW, Room B3–221, Washington, DC.

Seamon, F. 1992. Intergenerational issues related to the crack-cocaine problem. *Family and Community Health* 15(3): 111–119.

Stack, C. B. 1974. *All our kin: Strategies for survival in a black community*. New York: Harper and Row.

Staples, R. 1976. *Introduction to sociology*. New York: McGraw-Hill.

STATA StataCorp. 1994. Stata Statistical Software: Release 6.0. College Station, TX: Stata Corporation.

Sterling, D. 1984. *We are your sisters: Black women in the nineteenth century*. New York: W. W. Norton.

Szinovacz, M. E. 1998. Grandparents today: A demographic profile. *The Gerontologist* 38(1): 37–52.

Szinovacz, M. E., S. DeViney, and M. P. Atkinson. 1999. The effects of surrogate parenting on grandparents' well-being. *Journal of Gerontology* 54B(6): S376–388.

Taylor, R. J., M. B. Tucker, L. M. Chatters, and R. Jayakody. 1997. Recent demographic trends in African-American family structure. In *Family life in black America*, eds. T. J. Taylor, J. S. Jackson, and L. M. Chatters. Newbury Park, CA: Sage.

Tran, T. V., R. Wright, and L. Chatters. 1991. Health, stress, psychological resources, and subjective well-being among older Blacks. *Psychology and Aging* 6:100–108.

U.S. Bureau of the Census. 1970 and 1980 Censuses and 1990 and 1997 Current Population Surveys as reported in Marital Status and Living Arrangements: March 1994, Table A-6 and Marital Status and Living Arrangement. Washington, DC: U.S. Government Printing Office.

U.S. Bureau of the Census, Current Population Reports, Series P20–574, Marital Status and Living Arrangements. Washington, DC: U.S. Government Printing Office, March 1998.

U.S. Bureau of the Census. Census of the Population. Marital Status and Living Arrangements. Current Population Reports, Population Characteristics, Series P-20, No.468. Washington, DC: U.S. Government Printing Office, March 1992.

U.S. Bureau of the Census. 1990. Census of the population. Marital status and living arrangements. Current Population Reports, Population Characteristics, Series P-20, No. 461. Washington, DC: U.S. Government Printing Office, March 1992.

U.S. Bureau of the Census. 2001. Grandchildren living in the home of their grandparents: 1970 to present. *Historical time series table CH-7*. Accessed February 21, 2003, from http://www.census.gov/population/socdemo/hh-fam/tabCH-7.txt.

U.S. Bureau of the Census. 2001. QT-02. Profile of Selected Social Characteristics. Census 2000 Supplementary Survey (C2SS) Summary Tables. Accessed February 21, 2003, from http://factfinder.census.gov/home/en/c2ss.html.

Utsey, S. O., Y. A. Payne, E. S. Jackson, and A. M. Jones. 2002. Race-related stress, quality of life indicators, and life satisfaction among elderly African Americans. *Cultural Diversity and Ethnic Minority Psychology* 8:224–233.

Velkoff, V. A., and V. A. Lawson. 1998. *Gender and aging.* International Programs Center, U.S. Department of Commerce, Economics and Statistics Administration, Bureau of the Census, December 1998.

Wade-Gayles, G., and E. Finch. 1995. The "Finny-Fanny" rain: Three women's spiritual bonding on Sapelo Island. In *My soul is a witness*, ed. Wade-Gayles, 00–00. Boston: Beacon Press.

Wallace, K. A. and A. J. Wheeler. 2002. Reliability generalization of the life satisfaction index. *Educational Psychological Measurement* 62:674–684.

White, D. 1984. The lives of slave women. *Southern Exposure* 12:32–39.

Wilson, M. N. 1986. The black extended family: An analytical consideration. *Developmental Psychology* 22:246–258.

# Index

**About the Author**

DOROTHY SMITH RUIZ is Associate Professor of African American and African Studies and Sociology at the University of North Carolina, Charlotte. She is also the author of *Mental Health and Mental Disorder among Black Americans* (Greenwood Press, 1990).